John Mitchell, who comes from Shipley in Yorkshire, has long experience in journalism (he was
for thirteen years editor of a local paper) and
teaching (he was Senior Lecturer in Communication Studies at Bradford College before he
became a private consultant). His special
interest in recent years has been problems of
written communication in industry. Most of his
time is now spent advising local and national
companies and institutions on report writing.
Mr Mitchell was educated at Huddersfield College of Education and Leeds University.

JOHN MITCHELL

HOW TO WRITE REPORTS

FONTANA PAPERBACKS

First published by Fontana Paperbacks 1974
Seventh impression, with minor revisions, September
1981
Ninth impression October 1984

Made and printed in Great Britain by
William Collins Sons & Co. Ltd, Glasgow

CONTENTS

ACKNOWLEDGEMENTS

I gratefully acknowledge the help and advice I have received from many people in writing this book.

To my students, young and old, in a variety of disciplines, inside and outside college, I am indebted for the stimulation of their ideas and the frankness of their criticisms.

To my colleagues at the Bradford College of Art and Technology, I am grateful for unstinted co-operation, especially to Mr E. McNicholas, who read the script and the proofs; Mr T. L. J. Keep, who provided the illustrations; Mr F. M. Jorysz who helped with information sources; Mr L. B. Horner, who checked the legal aspects; Mr J. C. Brown and his civil engineering students, who produced the check list for a technical investigation report.

To the following, I am indebted for permission to reproduce extracts and examples: The Director of the Building Research Establishment, Department of the Environment, Watford, for permission to reproduce Digest No. 113; W. C. Holmes and Company Ltd., chemical and mechanical plant manufacturers, Huddersfield, for their example of an inspection report; Mr T. M. Smith, Area Training Officer, Post Office Telephones, Bradford, for permission to reproduce the title page of one of his reports; Mr D. B. Roberts, of Garnet-Bywater Ltd., Cleck-heaton, for his contents list.

To my wife, Phyllis, I am, as ever, indebted for secretarial help and for typing the script.

J.M.

SECTION 1

INTRODUCTION

I DEFINITION

A technical report is a written statement of the facts of a situation, project, process or test; how these facts were ascertained; their significance; the conclusions that have been drawn from them; the recommendations[1] that are being made.

1. *Note:* Recommendations are not required in all cases.

II WHY WRITE REPORTS?

1. A NECESSITY

Technical reports are a necessity. The storage and analysis of information in reports is essential to the functioning of modern industry and undoubtedly plays a part in its expansion.

Reports are needed to:

(*a*) record work done, whether conclusive or not;

(*b*) assess a situation;

(*c*) test the validity of information;

(*d*) avoid repeating work already done;

(*e*) circulate new ideas;

(*f*) provide means of cross-fertilisation of ideas;

(*g*) indicate a course of action to be taken as a result of work done;

(*h*) keep others, especially management, informed of work done and of progress made.

2. REASONS

In the minds of those who have to write reports, the reasons for doing so vary. Principal among them are:

(*a*) to supply the reader with the information he needs in a form he can understand;

(*b*) to please the Boss or the Tutor;

(*c*) to justify one's place, position or existence in the firm, establishment or college.

Looked at objectively, only the first of these three reasons is valid. Reports are (or should be) written primarily to inform, not to impress. But, of course, a good report, logically, clearly and concisely presented according to the needs of the particular readership, often creates a good impression that can only enhance the reputation of the writer. The report is the crown of a person's technical achievement, and the means whereby the quality of his work is judged. Therefore the techniques of report writing merit the most careful attention.

3. COMMON FALLACIES

The importance of the subject, however, should not blind report writers to the fallacies commonly held among those who call for and who write reports. Among these fallacies are:

(*a*) that staff actually enjoy writing reports;

(*b*) that superiors usually enjoy reading them;

(*c*) that the largeness of a report is bound to impress the reader (i.e. that its importance is in direct ratio to its weight);

(*d*) that the only safe way is to give the reader all the facts and let him sort them out for himself;

(*e*) that report writing requires something other than plain, straightforward, unadorned English;

(*f*) that a report is the only way of presenting the information.

In the 20th century we are suffering an information explosion the like of which has never been experienced before. Every manager is being inundated with piles of reading matter that he has no time to read, let alone to digest.

The purpose of this book is *not* to increase the piles of paper with which he is surrounded. Reports that will never be used, and that no one has the time to read, are a waste of valuable time, as also are long reports when only an abstract or digest is needed. Notes, memos, charts and illustrations are other ways of presenting information in a quickly and easily assimilated form. The report should, therefore, be reserved for real need and then presented with economy in the amount of information given.

SECTION 2

PRODUCING A REPORT

1 A SYSTEMATIC APPROACH

The production of a report divides logically into the following stages:

    (*a*) instructions;

    (*b*) preparation;

    (*c*) classification;

    (*d*) planning and layout;

    (*e*) writing;

    (*f*) review.

None of these stages should be omitted. Many writers, in their desire to get on with the job, prefer to start with item (*e*), in the hope that the report will somehow sort itself out as they go along. Seldom is such an approach successful. Indeed, such a report can only be efficient where the writer already has all the necessary information in his head and where, mentally at least, he has already gone through the stages outlined.

The secret of successful report writing is a systematic approach. One does not have to be a literary genius to write good reports, but one does have to be a tidy thinker who presents his material simply, clearly and logically. A step-by-step approach to report writing makes clear presentation easier and saves the time of writer and reader alike.

II INSTRUCTIONS

1. TERMS OF REFERENCE

Clear, agreed instructions are the foundation upon which a report is built. Where they are provided, the technical name for them is Terms of Reference. They outline the objectives of the report and of the work that precedes it. For example, a committee of inquiry is always given specific instructions as to the subject of its considerations, and both the extent and the limitations of the inquiry to be made. The committee, having come to its findings, will then quote the Terms of Reference in its report. In the same way, many kinds of tests undertaken in industry have precise and predetermined objectives which, in their turn, become the Terms of Reference quoted in the report when the tests have been completed.

Terms of Reference define the scope of a report and the lines the writer is required to follow. They outline the aspects to be considered and indicate the limitations to be observed. For example, a mail order firm interested in the possibilities of expansion in the Common Market might instruct its sales manager to produce a report for which the terms of reference might be:

To report on current mail order businesses and practices in Europe, the extent of their operations, turnover and clientele; mail order charges in Europe and any restrictions on imports across national boundaries; local taxation; the possibility of establishing warehouse and despatch facilities in Europe; lines most attractive to the Continental buyer and the organisation necessary to produce the firm's catalogues in several European languages.

Some kinds of report are called for so frequently and are so stereotyped in their requirements as to make it possible for the writer to be provided with headings under which the various parts are to be written. Such pro forma reports have their own Terms of Reference built into them and are usually easy to follow. The danger is, however, that some of the headings may be inadequate as guides to what is really needed, and they may not cater for variations from the norm. Where reports are frequently called for along similar, but not precisely the same, lines, the best way to meet the problem of guiding the writer is to produce a check list. Methods of preparing check lists will be considered later (p. 92).

2. THESIS SENTENCE

All too frequently, the writer of a report is given neither Terms of Reference nor printed guide lines. Instead, he receives a vague directive, such as, 'Oh, Mr Brown, give me a report on Fire Precautions, will you?' Not wishing to appear inadequate, Mr Brown assents and departs, still wondering what he is supposed to do. What, in fact, does the Boss want? Is it:

    (*a*) a list of the firm's fire-fighting equipment?

    (*b*) a report on the frequency and extent of drills?

    (*c*) a review of the alarm system and of instructions to the staff?

    (*d*) a survey of the fire escapes?

    (*e*) consultations with the local fire service?

    (*f*) a totally new scheme incorporating the latest equipment and warning devices?

How far does the Boss want Mr Brown to go? The amount of work required to deal with the various facets outlined above varies considerably, and to tackle some of them, if they are not wanted, would be a great waste of time. Obviously, Mr Brown would be unwise to proceed without clarifying his instructions. If, however, he is what the Scots call 'canny', he will not barge into the Boss's office to ask him straight out what he wants, but will first sit down quietly and write his own version of what he thinks the report should be about. Such a summary, when it is written by the writer of the report, is called a Thesis Sentence.

Mr Brown, who knows both his Boss and the fire-fighting set-up in the firm fairly well, might produce a Thesis Sentence somewhat as follows:

'This is a report on the most suitable fire-alarm, fire-escape and fire-prevention system for the Springbank Works of Alfred Troutman and Sons Ltd., the cost of installation and of any structural alterations that may be necessary.'

Armed with his piece of paper, Mr Brown then pays his Boss a visit and after suitable politeness, asks him: 'About the fire precautions report. Would you want it along these lines?'

Admittedly, by his action Mr Brown has laid himself open to criticism. He may even be accused of stupidly misinterpreting the situation. That is a risk he has to take. It would be far worse, however, to waste much time seeking, producing and writing up information that is not needed and to incur the wrath of his superior in that way. Unless the Thesis Sentence is very wide of the mark, reaction is likely to be favourable. The probabilities are that Mr Brown will either:

(a) receive 'the green light' to carry on with the report as outlined in the Thesis Sentence with, perhaps, minor modifications, or

(b) induce the Boss to commit himself in writing and state exactly what he requires.

The Thesis Sentence has now become not merely a test of the writer's comprehension of the report, but also an agreed basis for it and a safeguard against changes of mind. Many months may elapse between the time when a report is called for and when it is produced, and the human mind can be both fickle and forgetful. In these circumstances, the Thesis Sentence becomes an insurance against future criticism. It is the Terms of Reference obtained by another route.

This is not to say that Terms of Reference and Thesis Sentence cannot be changed. Many a Court of Inquiry has had its terms of reference widened as a result of what it has found, and the scope of many a report has been widened for similar reasons. The widening is done by agreement and the report will then conform to its extended terms.

From the point of view of the writer of the report, sound Terms of Reference or a clear and agreed Thesis Sentence become the compass that enables him constantly to check his position in relation to his subject. They prevent him from wandering in the wilderness of the uncertain, the uncalled for and the obscure.

III KNOWING THE READER

1. COMMUNICATION

Communication is the art of passing on to others the information they need in a form they can understand. This definition underlines the part the reader must play in the writing of a report. The reader should not be a dim, shadowy figure lurking hazily at the back of the writer's mind; he should be considered from the moment a report is called for to the time when it is presented.

A principal difference between writing in school and writing in industry is that the writer is no longer merely trying to please 'Sir'. He is trying to communicate with third parties who are often remote from the Boss, or the office, or even from the firm or organisation. Obviously the report must be produced to the satisfaction of the superior, whoever he may be, but the superior is often not the person to whom the information is to be sent. Business letters are an example of this. They are written for the information of clients and of customers, not of the office manager. And however well the office manager may understand what is in the letter, it will have failed in its purpose if it does not similarly enlighten the customer.

Likewise the report. Some reports are written specifically to enlighten the Boss. He is the reader whose understanding has to be borne in mind when the report is written. Many reports, however, are written for outsiders, and it is the outsiders' needs and not the approbation of the Boss that must be the paramount consideration when the report is being written.

2. QUESTIONS TO ASK

Before the writer puts pen to paper he should ask himself the following questions:

(a) who will read my report?

(*b*) what does he already know (i) educationally? (ii) technically?

(*c*) what does he need to know?

(*d*) how best can I impart the information he needs in a form
that he can understand?

The answers to some of these may not be easy or clear-cut. A
report may not be intended for one reader, or even for one class
of reader. It may not eventually be treated as an entity, but be
combined with other reports to produce, under skilled editorship,
a composite report. Nevertheless, the effort must be made to
define the readership before work on the report is begun. Perhaps,
having made the effort, the writer may feel that all he has achieved
is a confusion of the issue. Instead of a clear-cut readership,
several readerships, each different from the others in education,
training and experience, have emerged. But at least the writer has
realised, before he begins, the difficulty of writing for so varied a
readership and he will go on to consider whether another form of
communication is necessary, or perhaps separate reports for the
several classes of readership.

3. PRESENTATION

When coming to his decision as to the way in which the reader's
needs will affect the presentation, layout, and language of his
report, the writer should have in mind:

(*a*) the reader's general educational background;

(*b*) his literacy;

(*c*) his familiarity with the subject of the report and with the
terminology likely to be used.

IV PREPARATION

1. ACCURACY ESSENTIAL

The soundness and reliability of a report rests upon the accuracy of the information presented in it. The collection of that information should be as thorough and as painstaking as time and circumstances will allow. There are certain techniques helpful to the gatherer of information that he should know and practise, but there is no substitute for meticulousness and accuracy in handling the facts themselves. Ultimately, a report can be no better than the research that has preceded it.

2. INFORMATION SOURCES

There are four principal sources of information:
- (*a*) personal observation;
- (*b*) the printed word;
- (*c*) visual aids and non-book media;
- (*d*) people.

Many reports rely mainly, if not entirely, upon the writer's own observations for their basis in fact. This is particularly true of laboratory and test reports, some aspects of which will be considered later. Upon the writer's accurate and honest handling of the facts depends the reliability of the report.

3. LIBRARY RESOURCES

The use of printed information in books, papers, journals and magazines requires access to those sources and some knowledge of how to use them. Every writer should be familiar with the library resources available to him. These may include:
- (*a*) local public libraries, especially their reference sections;
- (*b*) academic libraries in colleges and universities;

(c) special libraries belonging to research organisations, learned societies and firms large and small;

(d) Government libraries, and the British Library (Lending Division at Boston Spa, Yorkshire; Reference Division at British Museum, London);

(e) local interlending schemes consisting of associations of libraries in a particular area to increase and to speed up library services to industry and to individuals.

A knowledge of catalogues and of library classification often enables a writer to find his information quickly and easily without calling upon the professional help and skill of the librarian – though these are, of course, available to him if need be. He should certainly understand the rudiments of the Dewey Decimal Classification Scheme, under which books on the same or related topics are found together:

DEWEY DECIMAL CLASSIFICATION SCHEME

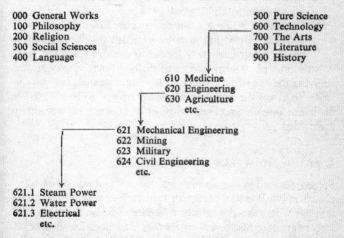

000 General Works
100 Philosophy
200 Religion
300 Social Sciences
400 Language

500 Pure Science
600 Technology
700 The Arts
800 Literature
900 History

610 Medicine
620 Engineering
630 Agriculture
    etc.

621 Mechanical Engineering
622 Mining
623 Military
624 Civil Engineering
    etc.

621.1 Steam Power
621.2 Water Power
621.3 Electrical
    etc.

The majority of libraries use the Dewey Classification. An extension of it is the Universal Decimal Classification Scheme (U.D.C.), which allows for more detailed classification. For example, a book on the welding of steel structures in building could have the following classification number:

$$624.014.2 : 621.791$$

in which the first part of the number (up to the colon) relates to steel structures and the second part to welding. The parts could, of course, be reversed if the welding aspect were primary.

All libraries, however, make it their business to explain to readers how their system works, and their staffs will gladly help the inquirer.

Books are classified on arrival in the library and the appropriate class number is marked on the spine of each book. At the same time, the book is entered in the library catalogue (card indexes or other forms such as sheaf catalogues or computer catalogues), which the reader may consult. There are two major types of catalogue structure. They are:

(a) *Dictionary Catalogue* in which authors, subjects and some titles appear in alphabetical order.

(b) *Classified Catalogue*, comprising a classified index, in which books are listed in the order in which they are classified, and two supplementary indexes for authors and subjects.

A little time spent browsing through the library catalogue and studying the classification scheme is seldom wasted. It helps the writer to assess the resources of the library and to be able to lay his hands quickly upon certain types of information when they are needed.

4. STANDARD WORKS

Some information sources are regarded as standard and as being always applicable to a particular subject. Every writer should be familiar with general works of reference and also those particularly relevant to his specialism, for they are among the tools of his trade. The following is an introductory list of standard works useful to the report writer:

(a) General

British National Bibliography: Lists all books published in the United Kingdom. Annual volume with weekly, monthly, quarterly issues. Dewey classified. Invaluable in the search for up-to-date information on publications dealing with particular subjects or topics.

British Humanities Index: Lists articles of importance from newspapers, periodicals, journals. Quarterly and annual volumes. Author index.

Keesings' Contemporary Archives: A weekly diary of world events, summarised from British and foreign newspapers and journals. Indexed.

Whitaker's Almanack: Information on local and central government, professional societies and public and private institutions. A most comprehensive general yearbook. Annual.

Who's Who: Compact biographies of VIP's. There are similar works for particular professions, e.g. *Who's Who in Engineering.*

Annual Abstract of Statistics: Comprehensive statistical information about the United Kingdom prepared by the Government Statistical Service and published by Her Majesty's Stationery Office.

Encyclopaedias: Including Britannica and *Chambers's* (for detailed and authoritative reference); *Columbia* (one volume) and the *Van Nostrand Scientific Encyclopaedia* (one volume), for shorter reference.

(b) Scientific and Technical

British Technology Index: Lists articles on engineering and chemical technology. Monthly and annually.

Kempe's Engineer's Yearbook: Covers all branches of engineering, arranged in sections. Detailed index with cross references. Annual.

Newnes Engineer's Reference Book: Similar to Kempe's, but smaller. There are also related works specialising in particular branches of engineering.

5. OTHER SOURCES

There are many other sources of information in the form of
published lists, registers, guides, etc., but two are of particular
importance to research workers and to report writers. They are
Abstracts and Indexes. Some idea of their comprehensiveness is
given by *Chemical Abstracts*, which now records information on
about a thousand journal articles per day. Such large-scale information storage and retrieval is, for the most part, computer
controlled.

(a) Abstracts
An abstract is a summary or abridgement of information found
in a book, journal, article or report. Often abstracts related to one
particular science or technology are published together, in sets.
Such information, already in print, is often referred to as 'Retro-
spective information'.

Abstracts may be provided by:
  (i) professional bodies;
  (ii) government departments;
  (iii) private commercial firms.

Some published abstracts

NAME	PUBLISHER	PUBLISHED
ANBAR (commercial)	Anbar Publications Ltd.	weekly
Chemical Abstracts	American Chemical Society	weekly
Government Abstract of Statistics	HMSO	annually
INSPEC Electrical & Electronic Abstracts (also Physics and Computer control engineering)	Institution of Electrical Engineers	monthly/ fortnightly
Metals Abstracts	American Society for Metals	monthly
R & D Abstracts	HMSO (Dept. of Trade & Industry)	fortnightly

Example of an Abstract:
22 082 A Cryogenic Temperature Controller. A. Tominaga.
        Cryogenics. Oct. 1972, 12, (5), 389–391. (in English)
A temp. controller for use with resistance thermometers in the range of
0.3–6°K is described. The bridge circuit which compares the resistance of

the thermometer with a precision decade resistor is described in detail.
10 ref. – A.S.N.
(From *Metals Abstracts*)

(b) Indexes

An index is an alphabetical or numerical list, or register, of subjects dealt with in a book, journal or report; or a publication containing a set of such lists. Indexes provide quick and easy access to information on research and developments in the many branches of technology and commerce. The information provided is normally the title of an article or thesis. Such information is often not yet in print and provides what is often referred to as: 'Current Awareness'.

Indexes may be provided by:
  (i) professional bodies;
  (ii) government departments;
  (iii) private commercial firms.

Some published indexes

NAME	PUBLISHER	PUBLISHED
British Technology Index	⎫	monthly
British Humanities Index (for laymen)	⎬ The Library Association	quarterly
Current Contents	⎱ Institute for Scientific	weekly
Science Citation Index	⎰ Information	quarterly
INSPEC Current Indexes	⎫ Institution of Electrical	monthly
INSPEC Cumulative Indexes (for Inspec Abstracts)	⎬ Engineers	2-yearly
Engineering Index	Engineering Index Inc. (USA)	monthly
Metals Abstracts Index	American Society for Metals	monthly

Example of Index item:

AIR TRANSPORT: *Traffic control: Radio: Satellites, Artificial, Communication*
IATA statement on aeronautical satellites. T. B. Wright, 'Flight', 99 (6 May
71) p. 656.

Each word or word group is cross referenced, e.g.:

TRAFFIC CONTROL: Air transport. See AIR TRANSPORT: Traffic control
(From *British Technology Index*)

6. MODERN AIDS

The use of television, microfilm and increasingly sophisticated reprographics is adding another dimension to the provision of technical information in the form of both illustration and the printed word. And computerisation is adding greatly to information storage and retrieval. Drawing upon these resources will soon be common. As part of his trade, therefore, the writer should familiarise himself with as wide a range of interpretative skills as he can manage.

7. ONE'S OWN LIBRARY

Much information is now so diverse and so specialised that it can be had only from the specialist library. Yet the private library still has a part to play in helping the report writer. Happy is the man who can turn to his own shelves for books that will help him in his work! What those books are depends of course upon his inclinations and his specialism. The young writer, however, cannot begin too early to build up his own library as an ancillary to his writing, as a means of widening his mental horizon and as a help towards the improvement of his style.

Also, on his desk, there should be:
(*a*) A good dictionary: e.g. *The Shorter*, or *The Consise*, *Oxford Dictionary; Collins English Dictionary;*
(*b*) Roget's *Thesaurus of English Words and Phrases;*
(*c*) Fowler's *Dictionary of English Usage* or Partridge's *Usage and Abusage.*

8. EVALUATION

Having found information, the writer is faced with the task of assessing its worth. This may not be easy. With his purpose and his readership in mind, the writer must sift carefully the information before him. He must develop a highly critical faculty for assessing three aspects:

(*a*) the intrinsic worth of the information, especially its reliability;

(*b*) its relevance to his project;

(*c*) its suitability for his readers.

The good writer does not reproduce information that he himself mistrusts, however favourable to his own case it may be. Nor does he exclude information from a reliable source that is damaging either to his findings or to his conclusions.

Where the bulk of the information is the result of his own observation – as in a test report – the writer is usually well aware of its worth and, often, of its limitations also. If the material is collected from outside sources, he must do all he can to check their reliability.

Points to bear in mind when assessing the value of material are:

(*a*) the standing of the author;

(*b*) the reputation of the publisher, and whether he specialises in the subject being considered;

(*c*) the date when the information was compiled or revised;

(*d*) the purpose for which the information was produced and how closely it is related to the writer's own purpose. (Some information has the chameleon property of changing its colour according to the background against which it is produced);

(*e*) the extent to which the information is supported by facts and figures that can be checked from other sources;

(*f*) the opinions of others who are specialists in the subject. (Reviews and abstracts are helpful here);

(*g*) whether the author is writing from his own experience or research, or is reproducing the findings of others. Information, like a river, is usually the purer the nearer the source.

9. REPRODUCING INFORMATION

Information may be used as a direct quotation (i.e. a word for word reproduction of the information); as a paraphrase or as a summary. In each case, the source must be recorded.

(*a*) *Direct quotation:* Where a passage is being reproduced word for word, the utmost care must be taken to ensure that the quotation is accurate. Quotation marks must be inserted to mark it off from introductory or other comment. Any breaks in the quotation should be indicated by a series of dots ... (usually not more than three).

(b) *Paraphrase:* To paraphrase is to say the same thing in other words, often more fully and more clearly. When notes are being prepared, any paraphrases should be clearly marked as such, so as to avoid their being confused with quotations.

(c) *Summary:* Often the most economical and useful way in which to reproduce information is in the form of a summary. Besides its shortness, the summary has selectivity and plasticity among its advantages. It can be fitted easily into the text, and can be moulded to requirements. In a sense it is a re-write and, as such, calls for considerable skill if the information in the original is not to be misrepresented.

(d) *Reported speech:* Occasionally it is necessary to include in a report what a person has said or stated. People seldom speak with the accuracy and conciseness with which they write. If a verbatim (i.e. word for word) report is not required, the gist of what was said may be given in reported speech, which may be combined with the techniques of the summary.

10. REFERENCES

References to sources of information are usually given in the following forms:

(a) *From books*

Author (surname, followed by initials); title; edition (if not the first); publisher; place of publication; date of publication; volume (if applicable); page number(s); section (if applicable).

Example: Houghton, B., *Technical information sources;* Clive Bingley, London, 1972; p 91.

(b) *From periodicals*

Author; title of article; journal; date; volume; page number(s).

Example: Ryall, P. C.; Low-Cost Traffic Surveys; *The Journal of the Institution of Highway Engineers;* November 1972; Vol. XIX No 11; pp 27–30.

At the collection stage, all sources of information should be recorded in case there is a need to check back or to explore further. At the presentation stage, some sources may be omitted to avoid cluttering up the report. The question of whether a particular reference should be given can be decided only in the context of each report. Considerations to be borne in mind are:

(*a*) The Law of Copyright (see page 78). The more specialised the information, the more likely is it that the source will have to be given and acknowledged. On the other hand, general information such as would be contained in a standard work of reference is not copyright. For example, there is no copyright in the facts of history; only in the manner of their presentation.

(*b*) The reader's needs. Will knowing the source of the information help him?

Note: When the source of the information is an abstract, both the publication in which the abstract appeared, and the original work should be quoted.

11. INFORMATION STORAGE

The way in which information is stored when it is gathered depends upon the amount and kind of information, and on the facilities available. Increasingly sophisticated methods from microfilming to computerisation, are entering the workaday lives of technical writers. For ordinary purposes, however, the choice is often between a card index and a loose-leaf notebook. The present writer prefers a loose-leaf ring-binder, with sheet refills measuring 22.8 cm ×14 cm (8½in × 5½in). This is easily transportable, easily re-arranged and supplemented, and not too bulky.

V NOTEMAKING

1. TIDY THINKING

If report writing techniques could be expressed diagrammatically by a pyramid, then without doubt the base of the pyramid would be notemaking, for this is the foundation of good report writing. Too often, notemaking is confused with copious accounts of proceedings and processes, or with scribbled jottings on pieces of paper. Such notes are scarcely worthy of the name – though they may have been the best that could be done in the circumstances. Efficient notes are characterised by:

(a) logical sequence;
(b) consistent classification;
(c) neat layout.

Tidy notes make for tidy thinking, and ultimately, for tidy writing also. Systematic notemaking brings one to grips with a subject in a way that listening or reading often fails to do. Notemaking forces the mind to concentrate, to seek after the logic of the subject and to arrange, or re-arrange, the ideas in their correct sequences. Notes are useful both for synthesising and for expansion. Practice in the making of notes is an essential part of the training of the good report writer.

2. THE SCHEME

Efficient notes combine clarity, conciseness and orderliness, all of which are aided by a consistent method of setting the notes out on paper. The notemaking scheme that the author of this book follows, and teaches his students to follow, is:

I. ROMAN NUMERALS AND BOLD CAPITALS FOR MAJOR PARTS

1. ARABIC NUMERALS AND CAPITALS FOR MAIN SECTIONS

   (*a*) Lower case letters of the alphabet and upper and lower case headings for sub-sections;
      (i) lower case Roman numerals and lower case headings for further sub-sections.

The relative importance of a part or section of the notes is emphasised by:

   (*a*) the letter or number sequence;
   (*b*) the size of the heading;
   (*c*) the position of the section on the page.

Within the scheme, the importance of keeping sections to their proper margins cannot be over-emphasised. Until a writer becomes familiar with the system, he should rule in clearly the outer margin (say one inch from the edge of the paper) and then pencil in the inner margins lightly with dotted lines, making the margins of equal width. The lines then act as guides, or prevent 'wandering', and serve as reminders of the boundaries to each section. On no account should a turnover line (i.e. the second or subsequent lines in a section or sub-section) overstep its own boundary or margin. Clear headings, suitably underlined, enhance the appearance of the notes and enable the reader to make a quick appraisal of them. If necessary, the pattern of the notes will help memorising and assist recall.

The following is an example of brief notes on pages 11-33 of this book, produced to the system outlined:

I. REPORT WRITING

1. DEFINITION: A report is a written statement of a situation, project, process or test. It includes:

   (*a*) the facts;
   (*b*) how the facts were obtained;
   (*c*) their significance;

(*d*) conclusions;

(*e*) recommendations.

2. USES: Reports are used to:

(*a*) record work done;

(*b*) assess a situation;

(*c*) validate information;

(*d*) save duplication of effort;

(*e*) circulate new ideas;

(*f*) cross-fertilise;

(*g*) indicate future action;

(*h*) keep people informed.

. STAGES: Production of a report is in six stages:

(*a*) instructions;

(*b*) preparation;

(*c*) classification;

(*d*) planning and layout;

(*e*) writing;

(*f*) review.

4. INSTRUCTIONS are framed in the form of:

(*a*) Terms of Reference (from higher authority) *or*

(*b*) Thesis Sentence (writer's own version).

5. READERSHIP: Before the writer begins he should ask himself:

(*a*) who will read report?

(*b*) what does he know

(i) educationally?

(ii) technically?

(*c*) what does he need to know?

(*d*) how best can I present that information?

6. PREPARATION: Thorough preparation requires:

(*a*) knowledge of sources of information, and how to use them;

(*b*) sound evaluation;

(*c*) accuracy in:

(i) quotation;

(ii) paraphrase;

(iii) summary;

(iv) reported speech;
(*d*) precise references;
(*e*) efficient storage of information.

These notes give the gist of the chapter, without the detail. They could, of course, have been expanded if necessary, but the overall pattern would have been the same. This is what makes the adoption and consistent application of the scheme (or one similar) so useful to the report writer. It is so versatile: he can use it for synthesising information; for summarising what others have said; for planning a report; for lecture notes; for public speaking.

NOTEMAKING EXERCISE

Readers who wish to try their hand at notemaking to the pattern outlined above are invited to reduce the information in the following passage to note form. Points to watch are:

(*a*) correct numerical and letter sequences must be maintained;
(*b*) capitals must be used as indicated;
(*c*) headings must be brief, and should not repeat information previously given;
(*d*) margins must be observed;
(*e*) identifying figures or letters must be inserted to the left of the relevant margin.

CLEANING EXTERNAL SURFACES
OF BUILDINGS
(Extracts from Building Research Station Digest No. 113, 1972)[1]

Deposits of dirt not only affect the appearance of buildings, they can act as a reservoir for harmful chemicals and can hide decay. The choice of cleaning method is important, for the use of an unsuitable one could result in damage. When selecting a method, therefore, the type and condition of the surface to be cleaned must be considered, in addition to the cost, speed and convenience of the operation . .

Cleaning methods
Water spray: Water is sprayed on to the surface only in sufficient

1. Reproduced by courtesy of the Director of the Building Research Establishment, Department of the Environment.

quantity to keep the deposits of dirt moist until they soften. Larger quantities of water are no more effective and may inconvenience the public; they might also penetrate to the interior of the building. Cleaning should begin at the top of the building so that surplus water will run down and pre-soften the dirt below. The time taken to soften the dirt needs to be found by trial; it could be anything from a few minutes to several days. In some instances the softened deposits can then be removed by hosing but usually it will be necessary to assist their removal with brushes of bristle and non-ferrous or stainless steel wire. For cleaning string courses or below cornices, abrasive stones may be needed. Heavy encrustations of dirt usually require careful use of mechanical means to assist in their removal.

This method is effective when the dirt merely sits on the surface or is bound to the wall with water-soluble matter.

Dry grit-blasting: Abrasive grit is blown under pressure at the surface to scour away the dirt. Some of the surface, particularly at arrises, will also be removed if it is soft or decayed.

Protection must be provided against dust and rebounding grit. Respirators of a high standard must be worn by the grit-blasting team and the gun operator must wear a well-fitting air line helmet in which a positive air pressure is maintained to prevent the ingress of dust. The air supplied to the helmet must be clean; unless this can be ensured by drawing it from some distance away, a high-efficiency in-line filter must be used. The helmet will protect the operator's eyes but other members of the team must wear suitable goggles or spectacles . . .

Except on isolated sites, the work area must be close-sheeted to reduce the dust nuisance, but even with this precaution escaping dust can be troublesome to the general public and to neighbouring properties. Door, window and any other openings in the walls must be sealed with adhesive tape and protection given to windows, lead rainwater pipes, electrical leads, and paint if it is not to be renewed.

Wet grit-blasting: This method is very similar to dry grit-blasting except that water is introduced into the air/grit stream. The water reduces the visible dust but the smaller harmful particles remain a hazard to health and so the same standards of protection are needed as for dry grit-blasting, as is the use of non-siliceous grits. The method is particularly useful when it is important to avoid dust nuisance to the public and to keep the interior of the building free from dust. It again involves an extra operation in rinsing down the surface after blasting, which tends to produce a mottled effect if the operatives are careless. Many operatives do not like this method and there is a temptation to turn off the water if supervision is inadequate.

Mechanical cleaning: The tools used include conical-shaped carborundum heads of various sizes and textures, grinding and buffing discs, and rotary brushes, all used with power tools. These spin off the dirt and weathered face in one operation. Hand tools such as chisels, brushes of bristle and non-ferrous or stainless steel wire and abrasive blocks (natural or synthetic) are used to supplement power tools, particularly for cleaning enrichments. Exhaust ventilation devices should be fitted to all power tools, or the operatives should wear high-efficiency breathing apparatus; eye protection is a statutory requirement. While cleaning siliceous masonry, the use of an air line helmet is recommended for complete protection.

Great skill is needed to avoid damage to surfaces being cleaned and to adjacent areas. Since the surface is reduced to some extent, the method is more suitable for plain areas than for mouldings.

Chemical cleaning: Most chemical cleaning agents either contain soluble salts or react with stone to form soluble salts. Every precaution should be taken to avoid contamination of building materials with soluble salts as this is likely to cause damage to the fabric: the effects can be continuous and progressive and the removal of salts is a lengthy and tedious operation ... These acids are extremely dangerous in inexperienced hands and their use should be left to firms employing trained operatives. The acid will etch glass and destroy any polish on marble and granite; it may leave unsightly marks on windows, pavings and footpaths. If it comes into contact with the skin, it can cause very serious and painful burns ...

Steam cleaning: Mains water is pumped to a flash boiler and the steam generated is fed to a lance through which it is played on to the surface. As with the water spray method, it is usually necessary to assist the removal of dirt with brushes and abrasive stones. Recent experience indicates that it has little to commend its use when compared with other methods, although it has been found that steam can sometimes help to remove deep-seated soiling after acid cleaning.

VI CLASSIFICATION

1. CONSISTENT SCHEME

As with notes, so with the report, there is a need for consistent arrangement and presentation of the material. Reports are not like novels, to be picked up and put down; or to be read and perhaps seldom, if ever, to be read again. Reports are works to be studied and perhaps referred to, in whole or in part, time and time again. Hence the need for the systematic classification and presentation of the information.

Good notes prepared to a pattern are the first stage towards the classification of the report itself. As headings and sub-headings multiply, there emerges a sequence of chapters and sections of the report itself. This then becomes the basis for the classification scheme for the report. Of course, the order need not be exactly the same as in the notes. Sequences may be altered, as required, but the pattern will remain.

One pattern has already been used in the notemaking exercise. It is by no means the only one available to us.

2. NUMERICAL SYSTEM

Some writers prefer to use the numerical system of classification (ISO 2145–1972E) as follows:

1. REPORT WRITING

1.1 <u>DEFINITION</u>: A report is a written statement of a situation, project, process or test. It includes:

  1.1.1 the facts;
  1.1.2 how the facts were obtained;
  1.1.3 their significance;
  1.1.4 conclusions;
  1.1.5 recommendations.

1.2 <u>USES</u> . . . and so on.

This system is the one adopted by many engineering firms.

3. CONSECUTIVE NUMBERING

Where, however, a report is destined to be used by a committee, or conference, a more convenient arrangement is to number each paragraph consecutively, irrespective of its relative importance in the arrangement. This enables members to arrive quickly at the relevant section:

REPORT WRITING

1. <u>DEFINITION</u>: A report is a written statement of a situation, project, process or test. It includes:
2. the facts;
3. how the facts were obtained;
4. their significance;
5. conclusions;
6. recommendations.
7. <u>USES</u> . . . and so on.

A drawback to the system, is of course, that some of the contrast between sections and sub-sections is bound to be lost – although this can be overcome by the use of various sizes of type for headings or for the introductory words to each paragraph.

4. OUTLINE OF REPORT

Having decided which classification scheme to use, the writer draws up an outline of the main sections of his report and, if he can do so at this stage, of the sub-sections also. In effect, he makes notes of his, as yet, unwritten report. By putting the outline of it on paper, he ensures that the report will follow a pattern to which full consideration has been given. He also provides a useful means whereby he can cross-check with the person who has called for the report that he is working along the right lines.

VII PLANNING AND LAYOUT

1. PARTS OF A REPORT

Reports vary considerably in their requirements; but they have commonly recognised parts. The number of parts a report may have depends upon its subject, contents and purpose. Attempts have sometimes been made to classify reports as 'short', 'medium' or 'long' and to specify the parts suitable for each. In the end such attempts are bound to fail because the requirements of a report are not dependent solely upon length.

What, then, are the recognised parts of a report? They include:
title page;
foreword;
abstract or summary;
contents list;
introduction;
body of report (which may have any number of parts);
conclusions;
recommendations;
appendices;
bibliography;
glossary;
references;
index;
illustrations.

Few reports would have all these, but the list may be taken as fairly standard up to the recommendations. Now let us consider the requirements of these 'parts' and their position and layout.

2. PAGES

In every report, as in every book, each page has two sides. When

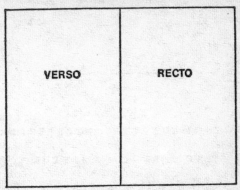

the report lies open, the left-hand page is known as the verso and the right hand as the recto:

Where both sides of each page are to be used, it is customary to begin each major section of the report on a recto. The title page itself, since it is the first part to meet the eye as one opens the report, is better placed on a recto than on a verso. In short reports, the title page is often treated as the front cover, in which case it is again a recto.

3. TITLE PAGE

The title page usually incorporates the following:

(a) *The title* which should convey, as briefly as possible, the subject and contents of the report. Long titles are to be avoided. If the scope of the report is wide, short phrases separated by semicolons will cover the subject, but writers should remember that titles are for identification rather than description;

(b) *The date* on which the report was presented;

(c) *Reference number* for easy reference and for filing;

(d) *Classification:* 'Secret', 'Confidential', 'Not to be published', etc.;

(e) *Author's name* together with his position and qualifications, as appropriate;

CONFIDENTIAL

ELECTROMAGNETIC INTERFERENCE
FROM RADIO AMATEUR
TRANSMITTERS

T.M. SMITH

Example of a title page, symmetrically arranged.

(f) *The authority* for the report, e.g.:
> 'Produced at the request of . . . '
> *or* 'Required under Sales Dept Instruction No 24, dated 1 April 1980';

(g) *Distribution:* A list of persons, or groups of persons, to whom the report is to be sent. Often the word 'File' is added to the list as a reminder that one copy must be reserved for this purpose.

Care should be taken to make the layout of the Title Page as attractive as possible. The reader's first impression of the report is gained from this page. That impression should be good.

4. FOREWORD

Forewords are comparatively rare among day-to-day reports. They are usually written by someone other than the author and are often commendatory, either of the work or of the research undertaken, or of the report itself. Short reports seldom have forewords.

5. ABSTRACT OR SUMMARY

More and more companies and organisations are stipulating that all reports shall have an abstract or summary. The purpose of an abstract is to enable busy people to get the gist of the report without having to read it all.

Mention has already been made of the 'information explosion'. Abstracts are one way in which executives can keep abreast of work that is going on without having to wade through pages and pages of material that may not be relevant to their need. But of course, if the abstract of a report whets the reader's appetite for more, the pages lie open for him to read on.

Abstract writing is not easy. Ehrlich and Murphy say quite simply that it surely separates the men from the boys.[1] The skill of the abstract writer is to give only the essentials that the cursory

1. Ehrlich, E., and Murphy, W., *The Art of Technical Writing*, Bantam Books, New York, 1964.

reader needs. An abstract is not usually more than two-thirds of a page in length, and it incorporates the following:

(a) *The Intention:* a brief statement of the purpose and scope of the report;

(b) *What has been done* or observed and how it was done – a very brief outline;

(c) *The findings;*

(d) *The conclusions;*

(e) *The recommendations.*

6. CONTENTS LIST

The contents list should occupy a page on its own and should be carefully laid out, with appropriate spacing. It should list the main sections or chapters of the report in the order in which they appear, together with their identifying number or symbol. The headings should be reproduced exactly as in the text and should be followed by the number of the page on which they appear.

7. PAGE NUMBERING

The numbering of the pages of a report begins with the report itself and not with the Title Page, Foreword, Abstract or Contents List. These latter pages are known as 'Prelims' (preliminaries) which, if they are numbered, are given a different set of numerals, usually lower case Roman: (i), (ii), (iii), etc.

The position of the numbers on the folios of a report is a matter of choice. Books vary on this. Some layout specialists prefer top or bottom-left on versos, matched with top or bottom-right on rectos. Others prefer a centre position, usually at the bottom of the page so as to leave the top of the page clear for headings. Whatever position is chosen it should, of course, be applied consistently throughout the report. Figures should not appear either in different places or in different styles in the various sections of the report.

CONTENTS

Example of a contents list.

8. INTRODUCTION

The introduction to a report may be likened to the backcloth on a stage. It sets the scene against which the action of the report will take place. The introduction may include:

(a) Terms of Reference;

(b) a short history of the case or subject;

(c) reasons for writing the report or for conducting the investigation;

(d) the name of whoever asked for the report;

(e) the scope of the report;

(f) the limitations of the report;

(g) the way the subject is to be treated;

(h) any special considerations that apply to it.

The introduction, though appearing at the beginning of the report, should always be written after the body of the report when the writer is in a better position to assess what is needed. The message should be brief – usually occupying not more than two-thirds of a page.

9. BODY OF REPORT

The body of the report gives the facts and findings, how they were arrived at and the inferences that are to be drawn from them.

The number of parts or headings that will appear in the body of the report must vary with the subject matter and the type of investigation that is being carried out. There are no hard and fast rules. Everything depends upon the number of facets the subject has, and the treatment required to give a logical and balanced presentation of the material. However, these things should have been decided long before one comes to write the report for they are part of the earlier notemaking and classification stages. If the preparation has been thorough, the pattern will already have been decided right down to headings and sub-headings.

There are some kinds of report, of course, that have standard headings under which the writer is expected to write his information. Among them are laboratory and test reports for which specimen layouts and even proformas are provided. Their weakness often is that they are too general if they contain only a few headings, and are mostly irrelevant if they contain too many.

A better arrangement is to provide the general headings and an accompanying check list from which the writer can cull or devise his own sub-headings according to the requirements of the report.

10. CONCLUSIONS

The purpose of the conclusion of a report is to gather up the threads of the argument and to present a considered judgement upon them. The conclusion or conclusions should be sound and thoroughly sustained by what has gone before. Nothing new should be introduced at this stage.

Some reports, because of the distinct facets that have to be considered in the body of the report, have what one might call mini-conclusions and recommendations at the end of each section. This is good practice, as it saves the reader having to refer each time to the general conclusions which may be pages ahead. But it does not mean dispensing with the general conclusions, as they are a most useful way of drawing together all the strands ready for the summary of the recommendations which is to follow.

Summing up should be:

(*a*) consistent with what has gone before;

(*b*) reasonable;

(*c*) clear;

(*d*) concise – and itemised where possible.

11. RECOMMENDATIONS

Sound recommendations are the hallmark of a good investigator. Often a report will argue recommendations that are clear-cut and admit of no alternatives. The recommendations are obvious, even before the reader comes to them. There are occasions, however, when several possibilities lie open before the reader in the body of the report and in the conclusions drawn from it.

For instance, a report on the line that a motorway might take would be unusual if it did not admit of alternatives at various points along the way. A whole host of considerations would crowd into the body of such a report. There would be geographical, geological, meteorological, ergonomic, social and even political considerations. Termini, access points and the best lines to serve the several conurbations along the route would be taken into account.

The balancing of all these considerations would require not only nicety of judgement, but also compromises, some of which might have to be adjusted later in the light of reactions to the recommendations. In such circumstances the recommendations, far from being ready-made, are founded upon clearly-stated facts, sound arguments, and an obvious ability to look at all aspects of a particular question.

Recommendations should be:

(*a*) sound;

(*b*) well-defined;

(*c*) concise;

(*d*) itemised;

(*e*) discreet, especially towards the feelings of persons likely to be affected;

(*f*) fully considered, including their consequences, which should be stated and costed, where appropriate.

12. APPENDICES

Appendices are for stowing away material that is needed to support the body of the report but is too detailed or too voluminous to be placed there. If, however, the material is needed to sustain the theme of the report, it should stay in the text; otherwise the reader will for ever be chasing back and forth between the body and the appendices.

True appendix material is that which the reader does not need to study in order to understand the report, but which he may turn to if he wishes to examine in detail the supporting evidence. It includes:

(*a*) statistical tables;

(*b*) detailed results of experiments;

(*c*) series of graphs;

(*d*) summaries of results obtained elsewhere;

(*e*) correspondence;

(*f*) lengthy quotations from outside authorities;

(*g*) maps, charts and diagrams.

Appendix material should be arranged in groups and labelled APPENDIX A, APPENDIX B, etc. The label should appear at the top of each page, followed by the folio number within the group: APPENDIX A - 1, APPENDIX A - 2, etc.

Appendices should be fully correlated with the text and referred to in the appropriate places, together with a word of explanation as to their meaning or significance. A reader should never be left floundering or uncertain.

13. BIBLIOGRAPHY

A bibliography is a list of works consulted by the author of the report. It has two purposes:

(*a*) to show the extent to which the author 'cast his net' in gathering information;

(*b*) to help the reader, and particularly the student, to find suitable background reading matter on the subject of the report.

The first presupposes that the author really has consulted and read the works referred to; the second that he knows sufficient of the sources available to be able to discriminate between them. For the way to set out references in the bibliography, see pages 32 and 33.

14. GLOSSARY

Every technology and every professional group has its jargon – most of it useful and much of it indispensable. To the outsider and the uninitiated, however, technical jargon or terminology can be unintelligible and frustrating without the help of a glossary, in which the terms are defined. Obviously, if the readership is confined to experts in the technology of the report, there is no need for a glossary. But where a readership is mixed and includes both expert and non-expert readers (as, for example, in Local Government reports, where both officers and councillors may have to be considered) due regard must be had for the needs of the non-expert.

If the number of words requiring definition is small, the definitions can sometimes be disposed of in footnotes as the report progresses, rather than in a glossary at the back of the report. When considering what terms to define, the writer should pay particular attention to those abbreviations which everyone understands except the reader. How can he be expected to know that, say, an ITA is an Initial Training Adviser, unless the writer tells him so? Sometimes the practice is to spell out the term in full at its first appearing and to use the initials afterwards. It is better however, to include the item also in the glossary.

15. REFERENCES

References may be dealt with in three ways:
(a) at the foot of the page on which they appear;
(b) at the end of the chapter;
(c) at the end of the report.

If references are copious, methods (b) or (c) are usually preferred. Where references are required in the text itself, the Harvard system is often used:

(Houghton 1972)

supported by full reference in a complete list elsewhere:

Houghton, B. (1972) *Technical information sources.* Clive Bingley, London.

16. INDEX

Indexes are required for longer reports to enable the reader to pin-point certain items or sections, and also to correlate aspects that may be dealt with in separate parts of the report. Indexes require thorough and careful compilation if full use is to be made of them.

VIII WRITING THE REPORT

1. THE BUILD-UP

Writing imposes upon us the hardest mental work that most of us have to do. If we are to write well we must understand the demands that good, clear report writing makes upon us and some of the difficulties that stand in the way of satisfying those demands.

Technical writing requires:

(a) the facts;

(b) the ordering of the facts and arguments in logical fashion and sequence;

(c) the statement of the facts in plain English, grammatically correct and properly punctuated;

(d) the supporting of the facts with adequate information and illustration.

A mistake that a writer often makes is to try to juggle with most of these aspects at the same time. He starts with a blank sheet of paper and the whole of the report in his mind – facts, order, presentation, conclusions and recommendations – and begins to write, trusting that all will be well. In exceptional cases, it may be so. Usually, it is not. There are too many things to think about at once, and the result is endless re-writing and much frustration.

The systematic writer builds up his report in stages. He starts with accurate Terms of Reference (or Thesis Sentence); collects the facts; evaluates them; make notes upon them; classifies his material; and decides on the forms and sequences of presentation. He comes to the writing stage faced, not with a blank sheet of paper, but with the skeleton of the whole report in note form – chapters, sections, sub-sections, headings and sub-headings, together with all the points to be made and the aspects to be dealt with. The major part of the presentation of the report has thus been accomplished without the least strain on his literary ability.

He can now concentrate the whole of his attention on expressing what he has already decided needs to be said.

2. EXPRESSION

Clear expression is not always easy but it can be made easier by following certain principles. There are no absolute rules, nor is there a formula for success. Writing is an art, and a highly individual art at that. A whole host of considerations enter into a writer's performance, including his education, background, vocabulary, experience, mental alertness, personality and his enthusiasm for the job in hand. These, collectively, form the reason why no two people ever write in exactly the same way and why most of us do not readily produce material of the same standard on two consecutive days. Yet we must achieve a certain standard if we are to be effective communicators.

Technical writing, unlike more exuberant arts (and unlike some other forms of literature) is highly disciplined. It is lean and spare and telling. The poet may use his licence; the novelist may exercise his imagination; the essayist may flaunt his high-sounding phrase; but the technical writer must stick to his facts and the clear statement of those facts. His liberty is bounded by the subject matter; his imagination is reserved for a consideration of his readers' needs; his literary flourishes are sacrificed for clarity and conciseness.

3. WORKING PRINCIPLES

The working principles of the technical writer require that he shall:

(a) always bear the reader and his experience in mind;

(b) choose short familiar words if they convey the correct meaning;

(c) avoid long-winded and roundabout expressions;

(d) normally write sentences of not more than twenty-five words, because they are:

(i) easier to write;

    (ii) easier to follow;

    (iii) quicker to read;

(*e*) use, for mass readership, the modern journalistic style of short paragraphs; for specialised readership, the traditional paragraph, dealing with one aspect of the topic at a time;

(*f*) prefer the active to the passive (provided the emphasis is right):

    Mr Smith repaired the machine (active)

    The machine was repaired by Mr Smith (passive);

(*g*) avoid double negatives, except where they are intended to express a neutral state:

    Resources will not be unlimited (double negative) = will be limited (positive)

    The workers were not unco-operative (neutral) = did not hinder, neither did they help;

(*h*) use adjectives and adverbs sparingly;

(*i*) not use emphasis words, such as *very, most, highly, extremely* unless they are warranted;

(*j*) try always to be specific and precise;

(*k*) not exaggerate;

(*l*) write to inform, not to impress;

(*m*) observe the three -FY's:

    (i) *Simplify:* keep to essentials and make sure the reader understands what they are;

    (ii) *Justify:* never make a statement or an assertion without facts or figures to support it. For the text to support one line of action, whilst the conclusions suggest another, is inexcusable. Where alternative proposals have been considered and rejected, they should be stated, together with reasons for their rejection;

    (iii) *Quantify:* avoid generalisations of size or quantity, such as are conveyed by the words *big, large, small, medium-sized*. State dimensions, amounts, weights, volumes as appropriate. The writer should not state that 'Profits are expected to double in the next six months' without telling the reader the current profit. He should keep any amounts or quantities in perspective. To write that 'output has increased by 50 per cent in the past three months' may sound impressive until the reader learns it is still only half what it should be. This is not to say that report writers are completely without guile. If to write, 'A saving of £10,000 would be effected' would be more likely to gain approval for a project than to write, 'a saving of 10 per cent would be effected', who can blame the writer for using the more attractive version of the same fact?

4. ORDER OF WRITING

As to the order in which the various parts should be written, it is often better to write the body of the report first. The introduction leads into it; the conclusions and recommendations rise out of it. The body of the report is the main part, and to write that first puts the writer in a better position to assess what else is needed. He sees more realistically the support the introduction should provide, and assesses more critically the conclusions and the recommendations that are to follow.

If this procedure is followed the order of writing will be:
(*a*) body of report;
(*b*) conclusions;
(*c*) recommendations;
(*d*) introduction;
(*e*) ancillary parts – appendices, glossary, bibliography, references, etc.;
(*f*) abstract.

The abstract is written last because, although it comes first, it draws the strands of the whole work together in a meaningful way for the person who has not time to read the whole report.

5. HUMAN REACTIONS

However logical, precise and factually correct a report may be, it will fail if it does not influence readers in the intended way. Many reports, if they are to succeed, must go beyond the merely factual into areas that affect human emotion and cause human reaction. Reports are written by people for people, all of whom have feelings about the coldest of facts and the clearest of logic.

The good report writer bears in mind not only the facts and the clarity of the facts, but also the impact of the facts, and is diplomatic, persuasive and, above all, sweetly reasonable in what he has to say. If his message may affect drastically work that has been done before; if it may result in changes of methods of manufacture or of organisation; if it may imply lack of expertise or of competence in the handling of a certain process or situation hitherto, he will be doubly careful not to overstate his case or to make unnecessary or uncalled for imputations against the work of others. Underneath the thickest of skins, there is a sensitive human being.

6. RE-WRITING

How often shall a writer re-write what he has written? The answer to this question must depend on circumstances. One cannot help feeling that much re-writing springs from inadequate preparation and from failure to be systematic in the build-up of the report.

Some report writers seem to glory in the fact that they have re-written a report, or a section of it, four or five times. Insofar as this reflects a writer's determination to get the report right, it is good. Insofar as it means that he regards re-writing as a fundamental and necessary part of the gestation of a report, instead of what it is – a great waste of time – it is bad. Nothing in writing is ever perfect, but the aim should be to arrive as close to the final draft as possible at the first attempt.

This does not mean that the report will be word perfect, or that a phrase or a sentence or two may not have to be changed in the course of the polishing process. It does mean that the writer has grasped the fundamental principle that he must first plan and think out what he has to say before he begins to write.

IX THE REVIEW

1. INDISPENSABLE PART

An indispensable part of the production of a report is the review. Primarily the review is the responsibility of the author, though that responsibility may, and probably will, be shared by other people, according to circumstances. Large firms, calling for many reports, may employ a sub-editor, particularly if the reports are for distribution outside the firm. Usually, however, the sub-editorial responsibility rests upon the head of the department or section in which the report is produced.

As far as the author himself is concerned, he will want the report to be as near perfect as possible before he hands it in for sub-editing. Unless he is being pressed hard to produce the report quickly, he should not review the report as soon as he has written it. At that stage he is far too close to his writing. What he needs is the distance of a little time so that he may approach the report afresh, this time as a reader rather than as a writer. If, in the meantime, he has had his draft typed, so much the better. For reasons hard to explain, mistakes hit the eye with greater force in print than they do in manuscript. Moreover, a typed draft gives a clearer idea of the effectiveness of the layout and enables the report writer to indicate improvements before the final typing or printing is begun.

2. USEFUL DEVICE

As with the preparation of the report, the secret of success in reviewing lies in being systematic. The report should not be read through only once, but several times, and each time the reviewer should concentrate on one aspect. Experience shows that a check list is useful. Some enlightened firms and organisations issue them to report writers to help them with the review.

The next chapter is an example of a review check list devised under four headings: logic, expression, punctuation, layout. It is not exhaustive. It may be adjusted or added to, according to the requirements of a particular report. The report writer reviews his work four times – once for each aspect – and considers the points listed under each heading as he does so.

X REVIEW CHECK LIST

1. LOGIC

How well does the report as a whole fulfil its declared purpose?
How well do the parts fit into the scheme and fulfil their particular
roles as follows:

(a) *Title:* Does it identify the report?

(b) *Terms of Reference:* Have they been adhered to?

(c) *Introduction:* Does it set the scene and provide sufficient
background information for the reader to understand the
report?

(d) *Body of report:*
  (i) Are the sections complete?
  (ii) Are the headings meaningful and suitable?
  (iii) Is the sequence logical?
  (iv) Are there any 'missing links' in the chain of thought?
  (v) Are any parts so detailed or voluminous that they
  impede the reader's progress? If so, appendices are
  needed.
  (vi) Are any parts inconsistent with the argument in other
  parts of the report?
  (vii) Is there a clear differentiation between established
  fact and personal opinion?
  (viii) Are any parts irrelevant?
  (ix) Has the reader been taken sufficiently into account in
  the presentation of the facts, observations, ideas and
  illustrations?

(e) *Conclusions:*
  (i) Are the conclusions warranted on the information
  given?
  (ii) Are they exaggerated in any way?
  (iii) Are they clearly stated?

(iv) Do they indulge in special pleading for a case that suits the purposes of the writer?

(v) Has the impact of them upon the reader been fully considered?

(vi) Are they libellous, indiscreet or unnecessarily hurtful?

(vii) Do they slander in any way other people's goods or services?

(f) *Recommendations:*

(i) Are the recommendations clear?

(ii) Are they itemised (where possible)?

(iii) Are they justified by the findings and the conclusions?

(iv) If there is an alternative course of action to the one proposed, has it been stated, and have reasons been given for the chosen recommendation?

2. EXPRESSION

How well has the message of the report been expressed?

(a) Are there any unusual words, phrases or abbreviations which readers may not understand?

(b) Have any long words been used that could be replaced by short words without sacrificing the meaning?

(c) Can any of the adjectives or adverbs used be deleted without lessening the force of a statement?

(d) Have technical terms been defined, where necessary?

(e) Are sentences short (normally not more than twenty-five words)?

(f) Are paragraph lengths suitable for the material and the readership?

(g) Are statements linked correctly to avoid ambiguity? (Examine carefully the occurrences of the relative pronouns, *this, it, these, those, they, who* and *which* to see whether what they refer to is clear.)

(h) Is the report in the active rather than the passive?

(i) Is there any lack of agreement between subject and verb, as in:

A programme of demonstrations were arranged.

(*j*) Has the word *thus* been used when there is no logical progression from what has gone before?

3. PUNCTUATION

Checking punctuation requires a separate reading of the report to spot the errors and inconsistencies. For a guide to punctuation see page 136.

4. LAYOUT

Good layout enhances the appearance and attractiveness of the report, as well as making it easier to read and to understand. Among the points to check are:

(*a*) Is the title page clear, attractive, complete and well laid out?

(*b*) Does each major section of the report begin on a recto?

(*c*) Have the prelims and the pages been numbered
  (i) consistently?
  (ii) correctly?

(*d*) Is the margin wide enough on both recto and verso, to allow for binding?

(*e*) Is the spacing between the lines adequate? Usually one-and-a-half, or double-line spacing on a typewriter is necessary to avoid too solid an appearance.

(*f*) Has the classification scheme been followed meticulously?
  (i) Are the sequences correct?
  (ii) Are the margins or indents consistent?
  (iii) Are the headings correct both in size and position?

XI EDITING

1. THE GOOD EDITOR

The production of a report is often a joint responsibility. The major part of the work is done by the writer; the supervision, editing and final approval are the responsibility of his superior.

The need for the superior to give precise Terms of Reference has already been stressed, but there is far more to editing and supervision than this. The superior who calls for a report and then ignores what is going on until the final draft appears on his desk is not fit to edit anything. The one who waits with secret glee his opportunity to wield the blue pencil is even worse.

The good editor helps forward the production of the report at every stage. He thinks in advance of the writer's needs; he checks the work without halting it; he directs without dominating; he encourages without patronising.

Far too many people edit as though they were bent on exercising their authority, or on showing their intellectual, technical or literary prowess at the expense of the writer. Their superiority in these things may be a fact – but they should not flaunt it. Such editing creates resentment and leads to discouragement. By his tact and helpfulness, the editor should seek to create respect for himself, for his judgement, for his experience and for his willingness to enter into the problems of the writer. Nothing is easier than to criticise. Nothing is harder than to rise to the standards of a superior who appears never to be satisfied.

Some editors seem to live in expectation that others can be taught to write exactly as they do. It is a forlorn hope. It is also a revelation of the editor's failure to grasp one of the fundamentals of writing, which is that it is an art and therefore a very personal matter. We all write differently because we are different. What the good editor seeks to do is to encourage the writer to produce the best of which he is capable within the disciplines of the subject and the requirements of the report.

2. HIS DUTIES

When the final draft of the report has been prepared, it is the duty of the editor to check it before the copy is typed or printed and then published. The editor should be as systematic in his duties as he expects the writer to be in his, and he should go over the report several times concentrating each time upon aspects worthy of independent consideration. These include:

(a) *Layout and classification:* Do they conform to the style adopted by the firm or department?

(b) *Technical content:* Is the research of the right standard, and are the facts:
  (i) as stated?
  (ii) adequately supported?
  (iii) consistent with the conclusions reached and the recommendations made?

(c) *Expression:* Is the report clear, concise and free from errors of English?

(d) *Punctuation:* Is the punctuation accurate and consistent?

These duties call for a certain expertise in marking up copy and in making corrections to the text so that the writer, the typist or the printer can understand them. Anyone who regularly undertakes editorial work of this kind should know the standard proof correction marks (B.S. 1219C), symbols and signs (B.S.1991), and the relevant glossaries published by the British Standards Institution for industries and trades.

3. WRITER-EDITOR RELATIONSHIP

If the editor, or superior, has his responsibilities in editing the copy, the writer also has his. Given the premise that here is a job that has to be done, what attitude should the writer adopt? There are some editors who give the impression that they alone know how to write reports, and there are some writers who seem to think that whatever they have written is well-nigh perfect. They adopt a prickly attitude towards those who have to 'sub' their copy and they withhold the full co-operation that the editor or superior is entitled to receive.

Understandably, anyone who has laboured long to produce a report will be sensitive about its shortcomings and will resent what may appear to be unjustifiable or trivial criticisms. Nevertheless, the writer must be prepared to listen to advice and to learn from those more experienced than he. If he is no better at writing reports than he was five years ago, he should ask himself, ruthlessly and honestly:

(a) Am I too lazy to make the effort?

(b) Am I too ignorant of my mother tongue?

(c) Am I too proud to admit my mistakes?

The aim of the good editor is gradually to reduce the amount of editing he has to do. The aim of the good writer is to produce acceptable copy.

4. THE SURROUNDINGS

Finally, while we have editor and writer together, so to speak, perhaps a word or two about the circumstances in which reports are written and edited might be pertinent. Amidst the hurly-burly of workaday life, men and women are expected to write and to edit reports which, if they are to be done properly, require maximum concentration. Yet the work is often accompanied by noises, distractions and interruptions that make concentration well-nigh impossible.

The harassed writer, or editor, struggling with facts and figures, with elusive words and with disordered sentences, is faced with the alternatives:

(a) of giving up in disgust and taking the work home. There, often when the family has gone to bed, he at last brings his tired mind to bear on what should have been done at the office. Then, bleary-eyed and far from alert, he re-appears at his desk the following morning . . .

or (b) of struggling on, trying to do two jobs at once, doing neither to satisfaction, and going home worn out and irritable . . .

These situations do not arise where management recognises that report writing is a necessary and integral part of the daily duties that staff have to perform, and that special conditions and facilities are needed, supreme amongst which are peace and quiet.

No enlightened management today refuses the tools, clothing and protection necessary for employees to do their work efficiently and safely. Why, then, are they so tardy in providing the right conditions for staff who have to concentrate on reports?

A small, combined library and quiet room, equipped with tables and chairs, should be at the disposal of all staff engaged upon writing or editing duties.

XII HOUSE STYLE

1. THE STANDARD

House style is the standard adopted by a firm, organisation or department to ensure uniformity in the presentation of information.

Style sheets, or style books, setting out these standards may be drawn up as a joint exercise by the members of staff who will have to use them (e.g. report writers, executives, typists, etc.) much in the same way as one would devise a check list. Or they may be compiled by specialists who have printing and publishing experience, and who also know something of the firm, its methods and products.

Compilation of a style sheet provides a useful opportunity for a review of current procedures and for co-operation by departments and sections in laying down the relevant standards. Rarely is a style sheet produced quickly (unless it is a copy of someone else's!). Careful thought has to be given to the alternatives and to the best guide-lines to ensure attractive presentation, uniform style and effective communication.

2. WHAT MAY BE CONSIDERED

Among the aspects to be considered when drawing up a style sheet are:

(a) *Format*. Shape and size of sheets of paper and binders to be used. Most firms have now chosen the A4 size for reports.

(b) *Layout and classification*. The arrangement of material on the pages of the report and the numerical and headline schemes to be adopted are the main considerations. Many firms are relinquishing the traditional, symmetrical style, with indented paragraphs, in favour of the left-ranging, asymmetrical style, in which paragraphs begin at the left-hand margin except where there are sub-divisions of the text.

Classification requires the adoption of the numerical system, or some combination of letters and figures, for the sequences in the report.

The aim should be to provide the best layout and reference system to make the firm's reports both attractive and efficient. The need to standardise the layout of title pages and of other prelims should not be overlooked.

(c) *British Standards.* Offer useful guides not only to letter symbols, signs and abbreviations, but also to accepted nomenclature in various industries and trades.

(d) *Spelling.* English is notorious for its spelling irregularities, including duplicate spellings. Among these are:

-ise	*or*	-ize
-ection	*or*	-exion
wagon	*or*	waggon
despatch	*or*	dispatch
enquiry	*or*	inquiry
cill	*or*	sill

(e) *Punctuation.* This includes:
  (i) sequences of quotation marks
  (ii) listing marks : , . - , or :–
  (iii) hyphenation

(f) *Page numbering.* Position and style.

(g) *Use of capitals and italics.*

(h) *Dates.* Styles include 9/12/73, 9th December 1973, December 9/73, 1973-12-09 (BS4795: 1972) etc.

(i) *Check lists.* For the compilation of reports.

Once a style sheet has been produced, a copy should be issued to all members of staff who will be expected to comply with it.

XIII WORKING WITH THE TYPIST OR PRINTER

1. COPY PREPARATION

The following are points to observe when preparing copy for the typist or the printer:

(a) Write legibly;

(b) Use double line spacing;

(c) Do not use red ink or red typewriter ribbon;

(d) Write or type on only one side of the paper;

(e) Use a catchline to identify each sheet as belonging to your batch of copy, e.g. Reservoir report; Re-organisation plan. Catchlines help quick identification should a sheet be mislaid;

(f) Number each folio, i.e. each page or side on which copy appears;

(g) Leave room for headings and sub-headings if they are to be added later. If the report is to be printed and the headings are to be 'set' on a machine different from that used for the text type, the headings should be written out again on a separate sheet of paper.

(h) Enclose in a circle any instructions to the typist or printer to avoid the possibility of confusion with the text;

(i) Observe house style;

(j) Make your draft as near final as you can. Time spent in retyping is costly, and 'author's corrections' to printed matter are very costly indeed.

Discuss layout with the typist or the printer and tell him what you want. Encourage consultation over queries or situations unforeseen at the draft stage.

2. CORRECTIONS

(a) Check the typed draft or printed proof carefully;

(b) Use the standard symbols for marking up corrections (B.S. 1219C);

(c) If mistakes slip through, or further amendments are needed after the report has been typed or printed, point them out to the reader. An errata slip gummed into the front of the report will suffice if they are few. Should the errata or amendments be many or long, it is sometimes better to interleave them at appropriate points in the report. Remember, however, that the impression given by numerous errata and amendments is bound to be that the report was not properly prepared in the first place.

XIV BINDING

1. IMPORTANCE

The binding of a report is important because it affects:
- (a) the appearance of the report;
- (b) its durability;
- (c) the way in which it can be handled.

All reports should have a binding – if it is only an extra sheet of paper, back and front, to act as a dust jacket. Depending, of course, on the importance of the report, the extent to which it is likely to be used, and the way in which it will be used, bindings can be varied to suit particular needs. They can range from sheets of paper, already mentioned, to professionally bound, hard-back cases with gilt lettering and as many trimmings as the budget will allow. Luxurious treatment is rare however, and all that most reports require is a neat and attractive binding in inexpensive material that can be attached in the office with the use of minimum equipment. What, then, are the possibilities?

2. FOLDERS

Folders are available in a variety of materials and with several kinds of devices for fastening the report inside. They tend to be clumsy, however, and often serve as dust covers, or holders, rather than as jackets.

3. STABBED COVERS

A simple method of binding is to take two sheets of glossy board (card) to use as covers, insert the report, and then stab along the binding edge with staples. If necessary, the stabbed edge can be covered with adhesive binding strip to enhance the appearance

Figure 1. (left to right). A report bound by side-stabbing (stapling), with the binding edge covered with adhesive strip.

Figure 2. A common type of ring binding, using a plastic 'comb' binder.

(see Fig. 1), and the cover can be decorated with titling, one method being the use of adhesive plastic lettering.

A drawback is that this binding requires wide margins because of the restriction it places on the opening of the report. Allowance has to be made at the typing stage. Remember that the wide margin is on the left for a recto and on the right for a verso.

4. PLASTIC GRIPPERS

On the same principle as the stabbed method is that using a plastic slide grip along the left hand edge of the assembled covers and sheets. The covers may be of various materials including glossy board, crimped or glossy plastic, or transparent plastic. These bindings present a neat and attractive appearance. Again, allowance must be made for wide inner margins.

5. RING BINDING

Increasingly popular in larger offices is the method called ring binding. For this a special machine is used which is simple to operate, and which perforates the binding edge, and then threads the binder (wire or plastic) through the holes in the covers and in the report. (See Fig 2.)

A big advantage of this kind of binding is that the pages lie quite flat when the report is opened.

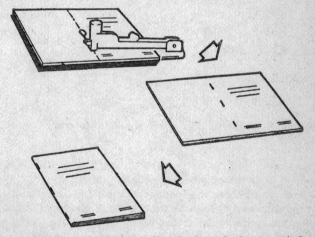

Figure 3. Saddle stitching, by stapling the sheets in the centre before folding.

6. SADDLE STITCHING

Where the report is made up of sheets folded in the middle to make four folios per sheet, it may be bound with staples, using the saddle stitch technique. This may be effected either before folding, by using a stapling machine with an extra long arm, or after folding, by using a saddle stitching machine.

There are, however, limits to the number of sheets that can be bound in this way without distorting the booklet. Care has also to be taken with pagination. A 'dummy' with blank pages will help the typist to get the numbering right.

XV LEGAL ASPECTS

1. DEFAMATION

Defamation is a risk all who put pen to paper run whenever they publish information or comment. The law of libel hangs over some writers, such as newspaper journalists, like the sword of Damocles. Over others, including technical writers, it hangs less ominously, but it is there all the same. Therefore, the report writer, in common with all other writers, should have at least an outline knowledge of libel and slander and, having been made aware of the dangers, should be ready to seek further advice as occasion requires.

Although there is no standard definition, defamation has been described as:

'A false statement about a man to his discredit.'
[Scott v Sampson (1882, Q.B.D., 491).]

'A statement concerning any person which exposes him to hatred, ridicule or contempt, or which causes him to be shunned or avoided, or which has a tendency to injure him in his office, profession or trade.'
[Capital and Counties Bank v. Henty (1882, 7.A.C., 741).]

What is at stake in defamation is a person's reputation, which may be injured either directly or indirectly. A libel need not be explicit, nor does the person need to be named for it to be actionable. Much depends upon the impressions readers have gained as a result of the statement. Does it convey to them the meaning that the complainant says it does? That is the test and it is one on which eminent judges have themselves disagreed. Where a libel is not explicit, but is implied, it is called defamation by innuendo.

Sometimes people can be defamed as the result of an attack upon goods or services they provide. For example, to describe materials as 'shoddy', or workmanship as 'careless', would obviously affect the reputation of the person or persons producing the goods or providing the work. Hence the need for the technical writer to exercise particular care whenever he is commenting on rival products.

In some circumstances statements affecting people, possibly to their discredit, carry what is called qualified privilege. That is to say that, provided the statement is made honestly and without malice as the result of a legal, social or moral duty, and also that the person who receives it has a corresponding duty, then the statement does not constitute a libel. Included in such occasions are:

(a) Confidential reports, properly called for by responsible people and published only to them, concerning:
  (i) organisations;
  (ii) management;
  (iii) individual personnel.
(b) Confidential testimonials supplied on demand by and to responsible people.
(c) Reports issued by trade protection associations for their members, giving private information concerning the finances and trading capacity of third parties.

2. LIBEL

Libel is the *publication* of defamatory matter in a *permanent* form.

(a) *Publication* is the passing on of the offending piece of information to a third party, that is, a person or persons in addition to the writer and to the complainant. Hence, to write a letter to someone defaming him does not amount to publication. But to have the letter typed by a typist, unless the typist is engaged confidentially on work that carries with it the qualified privilege outlined in 1 (a), (b) or (c) above, would amount to publication, for she has become a 'third party' – as has anyone else who sees the letter. For the purposes of the law, however, the spouse of the writer of the communication does not amount to a 'third party'.
(b) *Permanent form*, for the purposes of the technical writer.

usually means written or printed material. It also includes:
  (i) diagrams or pictures;
  (ii) models;
  (iii) effigies or likenesses.
Libel is actionable without proof that actual damage has been suffered.

(*a*) *The plaintiff* must prove:
   (i) publication – to a third person;
   (ii) that the matter complained of is defamatory;
   (iii) that such matter has been understood to refer to him.

(*b*) *Defences* include:
   (i) *Justification:* that the statement is true in substance and in fact;
   (ii) *Fair Comment:* that the statement was made in good faith and without malice on a matter of public concern;
   (iii) *Qualified Privilege* – includes confidential reports, as already outlined;
   (iv) *Apology,* either published or offered. This is not a total defence but may mitigate damages;
   (v) *Decease of Plaintiff* – on the grounds that the dead cannot be libelled.

Not only individuals, but also groups of persons who have been defamed as a group (e.g. a corporation, an incorporated company) can sue for damages on the grounds that their individual reputations have been defamed.

3. CRIMINAL LIBEL

Where the publication of a defamatory libel is calculated to cause a breach of the peace it becomes a criminal offence. In practice, criminal proceedings for libel are rare.

4. SLANDER

The defaming of a person in some transient or impermanent form, such as by the spoken word, or by gestures. Slander is therefore of little interest to the report writer whose work is 'permanent'.

Not all slanders, however, defame people or are impermanent. There are other forms.

5. OTHER FORMS OF SLANDER

Other forms of slander, which may be in permanent form, are:
  (a) slander of title (i.e. entitlement to property or estate);
  (b) slander of goods;
  (c) malicious falsehood.
These cover cases where a person's character is not defamed, but where false and malicious attack is made upon his goods or property as a result of which he suffers monetary loss. Actual damage need not be proved in such cases if the slander is in permanent form.

Report writers should be especially careful regarding the imputation of defects to the goods of others, and should ensure that all statements they may write regarding firms and their trading positions are accurate and are worded with the utmost care. The praising of one's own goods or products, known as 'puffing', is not actionable.

6. COPYRIGHT

The author's right of ownership over his original work, and of authorising what shall be done with it. Its duration is:
  (a) during the lifetime of the author, plus fifty years from the end of the calendar year in which he died;
  (b) in the case of joint authorship, fifty years after the death of the first to die, or during the lifetime of the author who died last, whichever is the longer.
After twenty-five years, provided appropriate notice of intention has been given to the author, a work can be reproduced on payment of royalties.

7. INFRINGEMENT OF COPYRIGHT

Unauthorised use of an author's work. Copyright exists in the way that ideas are expressed, rather than in the ideas themselves. It is not necessary to use an author's actual words to infringe his copyright. A summary or a paraphrase may be an infringement.

Points to note are:

(a) *Fair dealing:* Section 6 (1) of the Copyright Act 1956 states that 'no fair dealing with a literary, dramatic or musical work for the purposes of research or private study, or of criticism or review, shall constitute an infringement of the copyright within the work.' It is, however, left to the Courts to decide what constitutes 'fair dealing'. Copyright cannot be infringed unless a 'substantial part' of the original is taken. But, again, the Law does not define what a 'substantial part' is. Writers wishing to use an extract should bear in mind that its size in relation to the whole work may not be the deciding factor, but rather the extent to which the extract gives the essentials of the author's original work.

(b) *Publication of extracts:* If a writer wishes to publish an extract from copyright material, he should first write to the publisher of the original work. Permission is usually granted for the reproduction of short extracts. If the extracts go beyond what the author and publisher consider to be fair, permission may be refused, or a reproduction fee may be required.

(c) *Publication of paraphrases and summaries:* Bearing in mind what has been stated in sub-section (a) above, a writer wishing to paraphrase or to summarise *a part* of an author's work is not normally required to seek permission to do so, provided that the use of the author's work is not excessive and that the source is acknowledged. When to seek permission and when not to do so is a matter for discretion. If in doubt, imagine yourself in the position of the author and judge whether you might resent the use of your work in this way. If still in doubt, seek permission.

8. COMMISSIONED WORK

The ownership of copyright varies according to the circumstances in which the work is produced:

(a) Where a writer produced the work in the course of his employment, his firm, who published the work, owns the copyright.

(b) Where a writer writes articles in his spare time, the copyright lies with himself, provided the work is not reckonable as part of his employment.

(c) Where a writer is commissioned to write an article or report to a specification and for an agreed fee, the publisher usually claims copyright. If the article is not to a specification, the copyright rests with the author.

REMINDER

Detailed application of the law relating to Libel, Slander, and Copyright in any given circumstances is a matter for the legal expert. His advice should be sought in all cases of doubt.

XVI ILLUSTRATIONS AND TABULAR MATTER

1. PURPOSE

In technical reports, text and illustrations are complementary. A good illustration will often succeed where words alone would fail. Illustrations arouse interest, pin-point essentials and help the reader to a quicker understanding. They also save much time and effort in explaining and in interpreting the information. In general, the 'why' of a subject is conveyed in words; the 'how' of it in a combination of words and illustrations.

When to rely on words and when on illustrations is a decision only the author can make. He knows his subject and his readership. Just as he adapts his style of writing to his purpose and his readership, so also does he adapt his choice of illustrations. It would, for example, be useless to illustrate a report with orthographic drawings if the bulk of the readership did not possess the skill to interpret them.

The aim should be to provide clear, uncluttered illustrations that concentrate the attention of the reader upon the essentials. This objective curbs the flourishes of the skilled and encourages the unskilled to use the comparatively simple techniques at his disposal. To succeed, an illustration rarely has to be a masterpiece or contain masses of detail. Therefore a little practice in the preparation of simple charts, diagrams, graphs and tables will repay the report writer and give him a much greater versatility in the presentation of his information.

the writer is required to follow. They outline the aspects to be considered and indicate the limitations to be observed. For example, a mail order firm interested in the possibilities of expansion in the Common Market might instruct its sales

Among the uses of illustrative material are:

- (*a*) to describe an object pictorially, including the labelling of the parts;
- (*b*) to show details of construction and layout, including dimensions;
- (*c*) to show sequences of assembly;

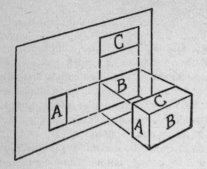

(a) How three views of a solid object are shown on an orthographic drawing;

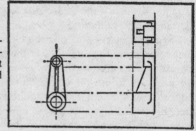

(b) The shape of this component, shown on an orthographic drawing, is not obvious to the untrained eye;

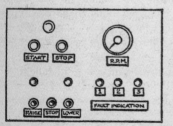

(c) This simple, 'flat' subject (a control panel), can be drawn and interpreted easily as an orthographic drawing.

Figure 4. Orthographic Drawings.

(d) to show sequences of connection, of operation, of processes;

(e) to compare values;

(f) to demonstrate logical trees, chains of command, areas of responsibility;

(g) to demonstrate diagnostic and checking procedures.

The author of a report may not always be called upon to prepare and to produce his own illustrations. In larger companies the technical illustrator or the draughtsman may do this for him. He should, however, have a working knowledge of the possibilities so as to be able to explain what he wants and to appreciate the advice the illustrator has to offer.

2. KINDS OF ILLUSTRATION

Illustrations are chosen for their distinctive features:

(a) *Orthographic drawings* are two-dimensional drawings, accurately scaled. Draughtsmen's drawings are orthographic and usually consist of plan, front and side elevations. Skill is needed to interpret them. Simpler kinds of 'flat' diagram can also come under the heading of orthographic. These are very useful and can be drawn and interpreted by the unskilled. (See Fig. 4).

(b) *Isometric drawings:* A pictorial method of illustration showing three faces of an object at once, but making no allowance for perspective. All lines that are parallel on the object are drawn parallel. The three main axes are 120 degrees apart – two of them at 30 degrees to the horizontal (see Fig. 5). The drawings can be fully dimensioned.

(c) *Perspective drawings* represent an object as seen by the human eye. Lines on the drawing converge the further they travel from the viewpoint. Most technical perspective drawings are drawn to two vanishing points situated to the left and to the right of the object (see Fig. 6). But they may also be drawn either to one or to three vanishing points.

(d) *Exploded drawings* show pictorially the items in an assembly as though they were spaced out along invisible axes.

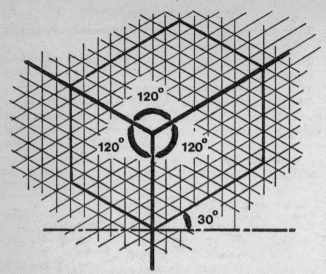

above The principle of isometric drawings, showing an isometric 'grid' with a cuboid drawn on the grid;

below An isometric sketch of a record player, showing how the scale remains constant everywhere. (Compare this sketch with Figure 6b).

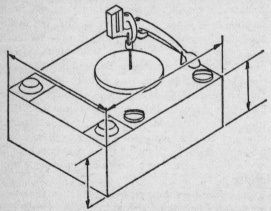

Figure 5. Isometric Drawings.

Exploded drawings show the position and inter-relation of the parts, (See Fig. 6c).

(e) *Schematic diagrams* illustrate what connects with what. They are commonly used for wiring diagrams and transport connections.

(f) *Cut-aways and sections:* A cut-away is a pictorial drawing showing the object with the 'cover' off in certain places, or with a 'slice' removed, to reveal the inside. A sectional drawing is an *orthographic* drawing of the object as if it had been sliced.

(g) *Graphs* show mathematical trends and relationships for the purposes of comparison of values and of calculation of intermediate readings.

(h) *Bar charts:* A simple way of comparing values is by using bars of various lengths, drawn to scale. The bars may follow a chronological sequence, as may the readings on a graph.

(i) *Sketch maps* are most useful to the unskilled illustrator as they do not have to be drawn with complete accuracy, or to scale. They are useful for showing the layouts of buildings, workshops, floor areas, car parks, position of machinery, etc. The reader should always be informed that the drawing is a sketch and is not drawn to scale.

(j) *Flow charts* show the sequences in a natural, industrial or organisational process. They are sometimes pictorial.

(k) *Algorithms*[1] are used for:
    (i) arriving at a correct decision by the progressive elimination of 'wrong' alternatives;
    (ii) preparing instruction lists;
    (iii) fault tracing, (See Fig. 7);
    (iv) carrying out complicated checks or tests without the operator having to learn the operational theory.

(l) *Photographs:* Unless a report has only a limited circulation,

1. A term used to describe both a Logical Tree (or Directed Graph) and a List Structure (or Branching Programme). It is 'an orderly sequence of instructions for solving a problem.' See: Lewis, B. N., Horabin, I. S., and Gane, C. P. *Flow charts, logical trees and algorithms for rules and regulations.* HMSO. 1967.

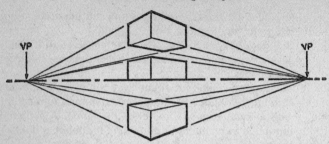

(*a*) The principle of perspective drawing, showing an object drawn from three different viewpoints. The receding lines pass through the same two vanishing points (VP).

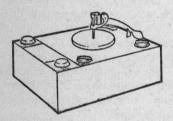

(*b*) Perspective sketch of a record player. (Compare the appearance of this sketch with Figure 5*b*).

(*c*) Simple exploded view of an electric torch. This is a perspective sketch, but it could equally well have been isometric.

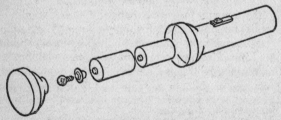

Figure 6. Perspective Drawings.

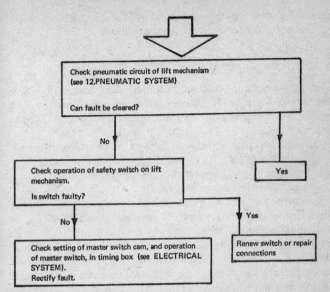

Figure 7. Part of an algorithm for tracing and rectifying faults in a piece of equipment.

photographs are an expensive method of illustration. Satisfactory reproduction of photographs requires sophisticated techniques and a high degree of skill, despite the rapid advance in office reprographic equipment in recent years.

(m) *Line drawings:* In general, line drawings provide better technical illustrations than do photographs. They can be shaded or highlighted to emphasise the points needed and they reproduce well without sophisticated techniques or equipment. Drawings intended for blockmaking should be drawn two or three times the reproduction size to sharpen the image when it is reduced. It must be remembered, however, that all parts of the drawing will be proportionately reduced. This reduction includes lettering on the drawing and the thickness of the lines.

All illustrations should be numbered, Fig. 1, Fig. 2, etc., and should be accompanied by a heading, or a caption, or both, telling the reader the point of the illustration.

3. TABULAR MATTER

This may consist of original or derived data, and may include ratios and averages. Sometimes tables are an alternative to a graph, where reading off the graph would not be easy. Tabular matter includes:

(*a*) readings of variables taken during a test or an investigation;

(*b*) comparison of data obtained with theoretical values;

(*c*) comparison of data obtained by various methods;

(*d*) mathematical analysis of results.

In devising tables, the writer should try to make them easy to read and easy to understand. If possible, the table should be contained within the area covered by the text matter on the page and be read the same way up as the text. Should this be an impossible arrangement, the writer can place the table 'landscape' using the long side of the paper to provide the extra width needed. Tables across two pages, and 'pull-outs' should be a last resort.

Other points to note are:

(*a*) Too many rules make the reading of tables harder, not easier. Often the only rules needed are those marking off the headings from the data, and the table from the text. If there is some distance between one set of data and another, a series of dots will help alignment. White space between the lines is a good substitute for rules.

(*b*) Text matter should be aligned on the left.

(*c*) Figures should be aligned on the right, or on the decimal point.

(*d*) All tables should be serially numbered, Table 1, Table 2, etc., and should be correlated with the text. A caption should be added where necessary.

(*e*) Where an illustration is to be used 'landscape', it should be placed so that the caption may be read by turning the report in a clockwise direction.

SECTION 3

COMMON KINDS OF REPORT

I FLEXIBLE APPROACH NEEDED

1. STUDY OF REQUIREMENTS

The techniques of report writing are very much the same whatever the subject matter. Reports are generally concerned with the statement of a situation or problem, the ascertaining of the facts, the presentation of the facts, and the inferences and conclusion drawn from the facts. Where reports vary greatly is in their subjects, their purposes and their contents. It may be of help, therefore, to examine a little more closely the requirements of some of the commoner kinds of report.

In doing so, however, one is acutely aware of the dangers of over-simplifying or of pretending to know all the answers. The more one studies report writing, the more one becomes aware of the need for flexibility in approach, in style, in presentation and, within certain limits, in the amounts and kinds of information given.

2. A STARTING POINT

The report writing considerations that follow are not, therefore, to be looked upon as definitive, but rather as a starting point from which report writers, from student to managing director, may the more easily come to grips with the requirements of their own kinds of report.

Many kinds of report have been omitted. Those that are given are among those the author has had to consider, along with students young and old, in college, in industry, in local government and in training organisations. Detailed study of this subject is still in its infancy. No doubt, as time passes and experience grows, an ever-widening spectrum of report-writing requirements will be considered and set down.

II STANDARD FORMS AND CHECK LISTS

1. SIMILAR PATTERNS

Although reports vary a great deal in their scope and contents, and have to be considered individually, many of them follow the same or similar patterns and it is only common sense to devise standard layouts for them. Two ways of doing this are:

    (*a*) standard forms;

    (*b*) check lists.

2. STANDARD FORMS

Where reports are comparatively simple and routine, a standard form may be devised to list the headings under which the writer is required to enter his findings. Routine maintenance or test reports are often set out in this way. (See page 94). The difficulty, when one is drawing up the form, is to steer a middle course between having too many headings and too few. If the headings are too general, the writer will often omit necessary information or supply information that is not required. If every possible aspect is given a heading, then space and time are wasted. Should difficulties of this kind arise, the adoption of a check list may be a better procedure.

3. CHECK LISTS

A check list is a list of items to be considered in writing a report. It is a guide to layout, to the kinds of information required and to form and sequence of presentation. Well thought-out check lists, intelligently devised and co-operatively used, save much time in the writing and editing of reports, especially in departments or organisations requiring similar reports from a number of people. The lists are not intended to be followed slavishly; any item they contain that does not apply to a current report may be ignored – after it has been considered. At any time the lists may be amended, adapted or extended to meet a new situation or a particular circumstance.

Where a group of people have to produce reports at regular intervals on standard investigations or projects, they should all participate in drawing up the list. A good method is to have one member write on a blackboard items suggested by others in the group. The first task is to set down the major headings in approximately the correct order. No doubt differences of view will arise as to relevance, sequence and terminology – but this is all to the good and will serve to heighten the interest of the group in the final list of headings and in the sequence in which the items are to be considered. The next stage is the sub-division of each heading into all possible aspects that might have to be taken into account. As many items as possible should be set down, even though some may be discarded and others may be merged. The process may then be repeated, if necessary, making further sub-divisions in the list.

Once the group are satisfied that all reasonable possibilities have been covered, a check list can be drawn up in conformity with the notemaking system already outlined. A copy, issued to each member, will then form the basis for the writing of reports by the group – until such time as amendment or revision is needed. Because each member feels he has played a part in drawing up the list, there is usually no difficulty in getting him to use it intelligently.

Individual writers will also find the check list procedure helpful, particularly where they have to write a certain kind of report at periodic intervals. Time spent drawing up the list for the first report is not wasted. Much more time is saved when later reports are written.

One example of a check list has already been given in the chapter on Review (Section 2, Chapter IX). Others follow as various types of report are considered.

RADER PNEUMATICS
MODEL E.F. NEW UNIT FEEDER INSPECTION CERTIFICATE

Batch No. _____
WCH. _____
Contract No. _____
Feeder Size _____
Serial Number _____
Radar P.O. _____
Date Due _____
Date Shipped _____

1. *GENERAL REQUIREMENTS*

a. Housing Material   Mild Steel BSS15/1
b. Knife Seatings are level and smooth   Sign _____
c. All welds descaled   Sign _____
d. Knife Cover fitted   Sign _____
e. Shaft Nut fitted and locked   Sign _____
f. Nameplate fitted and stamped correct   Sign _____
g. Painted   Colour _____ Type _____

2. *HOUSING*

a. Bore dia. before Chrome Plate   _____ Inches _____ m/m
b. Bore dia. after Chrome Plate   _____ Inches _____ m/m
c. Bore dia. (when supplied unplated)   _____ Inches _____ m/m
d. Bottom Flange level   Sign _____

3. ROTOR

		Inches	m/m
a.	Rotor Outside dia.	_____	_____
b.	Taper lock bushes tight	Sign-	
c.	Blade edges relieved	Sign-	
d.	Tips	Plain/Hard Faced/Removable.	

4. ASSEMBLY

a.	Bearing Clearance adjusted	Sign-
b.	Packing and Lantern Rings adjusted	Sign-
c.	Brass Seals Clearance adjusted	Sign-
d.	Lock Nuts on adjusting screws tightened	Sign-
e.	Grease Fittings installed	Sign-
f.	Bearing and Lantern Rings greased	Sign-

5. KNIVES

a.	Top Knife Clearance Angle correct	Sign-
b.	Bottom Knife Clearance Angle correct	Sign-

6. CLEARANCE DETAILS

			Inches	m/m
a.	Rotor to Housing (Top)		Inches	m/m
b.	Rotor to Housing (Bottom)		Inches	m/m
c.	Rotor to Top Knife		Inches	m/m
d.	Rotor to Bottom Knife		Inches	m/m

7. PREPARED FOR SHIPPING

Date_____ Sign_____

Inspector's Sign_____

Chief Inspector's Sign_____

A standard form for an inspection report (reproduced by courtesy of W. C. Holmes & Co. Ltd.)

III LABORATORY REPORTS

1. COLLEGE WORK

College laboratory work enables the student to:
  (a) test the theory he has learned in class;
  (b) improve his practical ability in dealing with set problems;
  (c) formulate conclusions from observed results.

So that he may do these things, and so that his work may, in turn, be tested, he must:
  (a) record the results of the experiment as the work proceeds;
  (b) write up an account of the experiment, of the findings and of his conclusions.

2. THE RECORD

Experimental results and any details of the experiment (such as equipment used) are recorded in the practical notebook. Most experiments call for a series of readings, which should be arranged in the form of a table, with headings. The units of measurements used should be stated. All readings in the table should be consistent – not, for example, to three decimal places in some readings and to only one in others.

The practical notebook is not a book on which to lavish time and attention, but it must contain an accurate summary of the experiment or test, and of the findings. All notes should bear the date on which the experiment or test was made, and, where barometric pressures are a factor, the time should be noted also.

3. GRAPHS

Readings, as well as being tabulated, are frequently recorded on graphs. This must be done as the readings are made, so that irregularities can be checked immediately.

The following are points to observe in drawing graphs:

(*a*) Scales should be carefully chosen, so that the curves will occupy most of the sheet.

(*b*) Normally, the horizontal or X axis will carry the quantity that is being controlled or adjusted, and the vertical or Y axis the observed quantity.

(*c*) If possible, the graph should be arranged so that it reads the same way up as the written notes. (Some graphs, however, have to be drawn with the X axis on the long side of the sheet, owing to the scale required.)

(*d*) If it can be assumed that the graph represents a continuous function and should therefore be smooth, without sudden peaks or changes of slope, it should be drawn in the form of a curve, not necessarily passing through every point.

(*e*) Where results do not follow a smooth curve, as in a calibration chart, they should be joined by straight lines. In this case, however, one cannot read off between the points as from a curve.

4. THE REPORT

After the laboratory work is over, the student has to present in the form of a report, a written summary of the work he has done and of his findings. For this it is usual to use loose-leaf ruled paper, and graph paper, and to keep the work in a folder or binder. Written work should be in blue/black ink. Green or red inks should not be used except for diagrams requiring the use of a colour code.

The work should be arranged as follows:

1. NAME   CLASS OR GROUP   EXPERIMENT NO.   DATE
2. TITLE OF EXPERIMENT: (in block letters, underlined).
3. OBJECT OR AIM: A clear statement of the purpose of the experiment.
4. APPARATUS: A list of apparatus and details of its arrangement, including diagrams where necessary.
5. DIAGRAMS: Diagrams should be clear without being fussy, and should illustrate principles rather than detailed con-

struction. They should have a caption stating what they are about, and, where necessary, be numbered and correlated with the text.

6. CIRCUIT THEORY (where applicable): A description of the theory *in the writer's own words.*

7. METHOD: An accurate summary of what was done during the experiment. The account must be written impersonally in the third person, past tense, passive voice, e.g.:

   correct: 'The circuit was connected and readings were taken.'

   incorrect: 'I connected the circuit and took readings.'[1]

8. RESULTS: All readings should be neatly tabulated and graphs carefully drawn.

9. CONCLUSION: The conclusion is most important as a test of the student's ability to reason from the work he has done and to summarise the knowledge he has gained. When writing a conclusion he must not merely state that 'The law was proved correct'; rather must he show the inferences he has drawn from the results obtained. These are expressed not as a personal opinion but as though the results were speaking for themselves. 'The readings show . . . ', or 'From the curve on the graph it will be seen . . . '

   Should there be a difference between his readings and the theoretical or calculated results, the student should give reasons for the variations, e.g. inaccuracy of the instruments used, the effect of humidity, variations in temperature, etc. . . .

10. LAYOUT: All reports should be written in clear, legible handwriting and should follow a set classification scheme. For the sake of appearance, ease of reading and systematic presentation, headings should be in capitals throughout; numbered or lettered sequences should be followed; margins should be carefully observed. All reports should have a ruled margin on the left, at least one inch wide, wherein comments can be made by the tutor or examiner.

1. Some institutions are now encouraging the use of the first person in the writing of laboratory reports.

IV TESTS AND TECHNICAL INVESTIGATIONS

1. WIDER APPROACH

Technical investigations take us a stage further in report writing. Much of what has already been said about students' laboratory reports applies also to test and technical investigation reports. The engineer or technologist is no longer engaged upon a set-piece, the result of which is almost a foregone conclusion. He may not even be in a cosy laboratory under close supervision. He may well have to devise his own apparatus and his method of working, and be sufficiently resilient and resourceful to change his approach and devise new methods as the test or investigation proceeds.

His whole approach is wider. Pure scientific or technical objectivity may have to be tempered, even moulded, by prior considerations of cost, convenience, climate, customers' requirements, selling prices, market surveys and a whole host of other considerations. Like the politician, he may have to be far more concerned with the art of the possible than with the pursuit of the ideal. For this work he needs a certain maturity of mind if he is both to perform his task and to write his report to satisfaction.

Some tests are mere routine and writing the reports is like filling in forms. But at the other end of the scale there are test reports that reflect all the technical skill, ingenuity and powers of judgement that their authors can bring to bear. High technical competence must be matched with high report writing competence if the work is to be recognised and the desired result is to be achieved.

Although investigations and tests vary enormously in their requirements, and therefore reports upon them vary in scope and in detail, such reports are all written to provide the reader with the following information:

(a) the PURPOSE of the work done;

(b) the METHODS used;

(c) the RESULTS obtained;

(d) the CONCLUSIONS drawn;

(e) the RECOMMENDATIONS made.

2. PURPOSE

The purpose of the work should be clearly stated in the introduction to the report. The statement may be limited to the intention; on the other hand, it may require elaborate background information if the reader is to be put properly into the picture. Among items that may have to be included are:

(a) the object of the investigation;

(b) the history of the case;

(c) the authority for the report;

(d) its limitations.

Although the foregoing may seem to add up to a considerable amount of information, the introduction should be kept as brief and concise as possible. Busy executives do not want to wade through pages and pages on the purpose of the report. They prefer action – and soon!

3. METHOD

Most readers will be less interested in the method used than in the results obtained. Nevertheless, the method is an indispensable part of the record and may be a piece of vital information if the test is to be repeated under the same conditions.

The method report includes the following:

(a) details of the apparatus, materials and equipment used; diagrams and illustrations should be included;

(b) the procedure followed – a step-by-step account of what was done;

(c) observations taken, recorded in tabular form;

(d) calculations necessary to give meaning to the observations.

Like the introduction, the method section of the report should not be overdone. Sufficient details should be given to enable someone else either to repeat the work without having to find out the whole procedure for himself, or to carry on where the author of the report left off.

4. RESULTS

Results carry the reader a stage further. With them begins the synthesis and the interpretation of the data recorded. Results may be expressed in the form of tables, graphs, charts, diagrams, or even bare statements of fact. It is up to the report writer to decide how best he can interpret, for his readership, the results he has obtained.

5. CONCLUSIONS

In considering his conclusions, the author must survey the whole of the work from its intention, through its execution, to the results obtained. Among the matters he may have to bear in mind are:

    (*a*) his results as compared with the theoretical;

    (*b*) results obtained elsewhere;

    (*c*) reasons for discrepancies or variations;

    (*d*) efficiency of the apparatus;

    (*e*) relevance of the method;

    (*f*) human errors;

    (*g*) environmental factors.

All these may affect the conclusions, which should comprise a mature and relevant assessment of the effectiveness of the work done and of the experience gained. The greatest care has to be taken both to draw the right conclusions from the evidence given and to see that the conclusions the author feels to be right are justified in the body of the report.

6. RECOMMENDATIONS

Recommendations in most cases will be the obvious inferences to be drawn from the conclusions. Where results show, for example, the clear superiority of one type of material or component over another of similar price and availability, the recommendation would obviously be that the superior should be used. Things, however, are seldom so simple or straightforward. There may be several possibilities, each of which has its advantages and disadvantages, and the final decision may be beyond the powers or the prerogative of the person who has carried out the test. All the writer can do is to indicate as clearly as he can the choice that lies before his superior.

Recommendations should be brief, but not stark. They should indicate the reasons for the action recommended or the selection indicated. Often a list is the most economical and effective way of doing this, as in the following example:

RECOMMENDATIONS

It is recommended that brick sample A be used on the Highfield housing contract for the following reasons:

(a) the brick is of adequate strength and durability;

(b) it has good weathering properties;

(c) it meets the requirements of the architect and planning authority as regards appearance;

(d) it is within the price limit previously agreed;

(e) the firm producing the brick has a good record for meeting delivery dates;

(f) the delivery offered for this contract is satisfactory.

GENERAL CHECK LIST FOR A REPORT ON A TECHNICAL INVESTIGATION

The following check list is intended as a guide to the presentation and content of a technical investigation report. Bear in mind that it is a check list and that it can be amended, expanded or contracted according to the circumstances and the purpose of the report. The order in which the items appear in each section is also variable.

1. TITLE PAGE

(a) Title;

(*b*) Reference;
(*c*) Classification (secret, confidential, etc.);
(*d*) Author;
(*e*) Authority;
(*f*) Department;
(*g*) Contents list (if report is short);
(*h*) Date;
(*i*) Distribution;
(*j*) Place where investigation was carried out.

2. ABSTRACT

A summary of the report with emphasis on the findings rather than the process.

3. CONTENTS LIST (if report is long).

4. OBJECT

A brief statement of aim.

5. INTRODUCTION

(*a*) Why interested;
(*b*) Definition;
(*c*) History;
(*d*) The conditions that had to be complied with:
   (i) Cost;
  (ii) Time factors;
 (iii) Environmental conditions;
 (iv) Required accuracy;
  (v) Political, social or economic considerations;
 (vi) Basic theory;
(vii) Any other relevant factors.

6. APPARATUS

   (a) Which and why (technique);
   (b) Description:
         (i) Written (sentences);
        (ii) Diagrammatic;
       (iii) Tabulated (listed);
        (iv) Limitations.

7. PROCEDURE

A statement of what was done (step by step).

8. OBSERVATIONS

   (a) Details of specimens, equipment, components, machinery, etc., during and after test;
   (b) Physical constants;
   (c) Readings of variables during investigation, in the form of:
         (i) Tabulations;
        (ii) Plotted curves;
       (iii) Diagrams (bar charts, pie charts, etc.);
        (iv) Written statements;
         (v) Isolated values;
        (vi) Photographs.

9. CALCULATIONS

   (a) Based on observations;
   (b) Based on theoretical considerations;
   (c) Leading to analysis of errors;
   (d) Summary of results.

10. RESULTS

Separate summary, if necessary.

11. COMMENTS

(a) Comparison of results with values obtained from other sources;

(b) Degree of accuracy achieved, having regard to:
   (i) Environment;
   (ii) Type of apparatus;
   (iii) Human error;
   (iv) Accuracy of calculations;
   (v) Possible errors in assumed constants;
   (vi) Time allowed to do test;
   (vii) Consistency of apparatus;
   (viii) Relationship with predicted results;

(c) Quality of test specimen, equipment, component, etc.:
   (i) Material;
   (ii) Workmanship;

(d) Alternative method which could have been used for presenting results etc. and why the method used was chosen;

(e) Further information sought or received during process of work;

(f) Acknowledgements.

12. CONCLUSION

Brief statement of achievement in relation to object of investigation.

13. RECOMMENDATIONS (including reasons for them).

14. APPENDICES

15. INDEX

V MANAGEMENT REPORTS

1. NEED FOR INFORMATION

Modern industry is complicated and interdependent. Thousands upon thousands of specialisms are needed to provide the goods, technologies and services that are part of 20th-century living. Even within one industry, or section of it, no one person, or group of persons can, by personal observation and experience, keep abreast of relevant information. All managers depend upon a constant and reliable flow of information which reaches them through various media.

Written reports make a valuable contribution towards this flow. The larger the firm or organisation, the more important the report as a means of informing others, 'vertically' and 'horizontally', of present situations and of future possibilities.

Among the advantages of the written report as a tool of management are:

    (*a*) its Terms of Reference can be precisely defined;

    (*b*) it can be thoroughly prepared;

    (*c*) it lessens the likelihood of premature and hurried judgements;

    (*d*) it can be widely circulated;

    (*e*) it can be studied at a convenient time.

Few kinds of report writing make such high demands upon the skill of the writer as do industrial management reports because of the many factors that may have to be taken into account. Materials, quality control, training, technology, human relations, plant, labour, competition, sales, publicity and finance are some of them. Thinking carefully through the implications and interaction of these requires painstaking research, careful appraisal, and clear expression, if the communication is to succeed.

Many managers find the report a final burden; almost the last straw. Viewed properly, however, it is the validation of all that has gone before, from the research to the recommendations. The report provides the means whereby the manager can check his work and his reasoning before he communicates it to others. Often the process of writing will itself discover the omissions and the flaws; for logic, both in derivation and in fact, begins with words.

2. EVER CHANGING

All management reports have to do with change. Even a report on a present situation is really a probe to see whether action needs to be taken. Industry never rests. Nowadays, movements within industry are continuous and accelerating. Automation is bringing about vast changes in technology, while computerisation is effecting a revolution in methods and control. The manager's part is to seek out the relevant information and then to present it in such a way that others may understand and, if necessary, form judgements upon it. This is a tall order indeed for a man who is expected to have his own technical specialism, plus a working knowledge of several others. Yet the fact remains that thought, however relevant and profound, remains useless unless it is communicated to others. An inarticulate manager cannot do his job.

3. THREE SUBJECTS

Management reports deal in the main with three subjects:

(*a*) people;
(*b*) organisation;
(*c*) hardware – goods, plant, materials, components, etc.

Reports about people merit separate consideration. Organisational reports are about situations and the problems they pose. Reports on goods or equipment are usually less complicated. All three, however, overlap because they affect one another.

To include every industrial situation in a review of this kind is impossible. Nevertheless an attempt to compile a general organisational check list is worth making in the hope that it may provide a starting point for others. Here, then, is a possible check list for an organisational report:

ORGANISATIONAL REPORT CHECK LIST

1. THE PROBLEM

(a) The nature of the problem and its causes;
(b) The extent of the problem;
(c) The effects of the problem upon:
    (i) production or efficiency;
    (ii) staff or workpeople;
    (iii) quality;
    (iv) plant;
    (v) training;
    (vi) sales;
    (vii) costs;
    (viii) safety.

2. THE NEED FOR CHANGE

(a) Industrial or commercial trends;
(b) Competition;
(c) Future roles and requirements;
(d) Labour problems.

3. PROPOSED SOLUTION

(a) Outline of possibilities;
(b) Details of proposed scheme;
(c) Previous experience:
    (i) internal;
    (ii) external.
(d) Advantages;
(e) Disadvantages – and how they may be overcome;
(f) Effects upon:
    (i) production;
    (ii) efficiency;

    (iii) workforce;
    (iv) human relations;
     (v) trade unions;
    (vi) sales prospects.
 (*g*) Time factors.

4. COSTS

For each scheme that is presented:
  (*a*) Implementation;
  (*b*) Running;
  (*c*) Estimated savings (if any).

5. CONCLUSIONS

  (*a*) Overall effects;
  (*b*) Overall benefits.

6. RECOMMENDATIONS

(item by item)

7. APPENDICES

(As required)

Note: items 1 and 2 of the check list may be reversed.

VI REPORTS ON PEOPLE

1. PECULIAR DIFFICULTIES

Reports on people present peculiar difficulties for the following reasons:

(a) Unless they concern performances that can be scientifically measured, they are bound to be subjective.

(b) Frequently writers are required to assess behavioural patterns that are likely to change according to circumstances and attitude.

(c) The words and phrases that form the jargon of reports on personnel are often ill-conceived, imperfectly understood and inconsistently applied. The present writer once reviewed a batch of reports in which the phrase, 'He relates well', was used repeatedly without any relationship being defined or stated. The phrase turned out to be a piece of jargon, which, to those on the inside of the organisation, meant that the man got on well with his fellows. The trouble was that the reports were intended to be read by people who were outside the organisation, and they were left to conclude the meaning for themselves.

(d) Guidance is often lacking as to the scope of the appraisal. The writer is left to decide for himself whether to reveal all when 'all' may not be necessary, or to reveal little, when more may be needed for the judgement of the case. Although there is a growing tendency to record and to store more and more information about people, there is still, in this country at least, a traditional reserve about prying into other people's affairs and a wholesome respect for the rights of the individual. The relevance of the information is the criterion. That a foreman may be living with a woman other than his wife may have little effect upon the role he is expected to play at work; on the other hand, that a proposed cashier has been convicted of embezzlement may be considered a necessary item of information in assessing his suitability for a post.

2. PURPOSE AND SCOPE

Both the purpose and the scope of a report on a person need to be defined. One needs to know:

(*a*) Who is going to read it;

(*b*) What is the purpose of the assessment. Is it:

    (i) the person's suitability or otherwise for a job, or for promotion?

    (ii) part of a process of continuous assessment?

    (iii) a statement of character and trustworthiness?

    (iv) a nomination for a particular assignment?

    (v) an assessable risk – such as probation, or parole?

Having cleared the readership and the purpose, the writer must decide those facets of the person's history, personality and performance that need to be covered.

3. PRO FORMA REPORTS

Where reports are constantly called for along similar lines, many firms issue neat pro forma reports listing the items to be covered, and perhaps gradations of each. Ticks and crosses may then be all that are required to settle the fate of the individual. If so, this would seem to be a pity, for men and women are not made up of ticks and crosses. All of us are complex personalities and something more is required if a pitcure of the whole man is to be given, even in the performance of a particular job or role. This is why a further section is often added to the form in which the writer is expected to give general comments on his subject.

Advantages of the pro forma system are that, where many writers are implicated, such as foremen, or managers, roughly the same information is obtained from each, and the amount of it is controlled. A disadvantage is that the report may become routine and perfunctory.

ASSESSMENT OF:	A OUTSTANDING	B ABOVE STANDARD	C STANDARD	D BELOW STANDARD	E UNSATIS- FACTORY	COMMENTS
Please assess each item: three ticks are required for each section·						
APPEARANCE: Smartness Tidiness Tastefulness						
ALERTNESS: Responsiveness Awareness Insight						
JUDGMENT: Soundness Imagination Experience						
MANAGEMENT: Initiative Control Experience						
RELATIONSHIPS: With superiors With staff With public						
OUTPUT: Diligence Consistency Speed						
EXPRESSION: Written Oral In conference						
STATISTICAL ABILITY: Mathematical Interpretative Computer experience						

Example of a pro forma report containing sample assessment items.

4. PEN PICTURES

Where reports prepared along these pro forma lines are not proving satisfactory, the answer to the problem may be a thoroughgoing check list. But because of the difficulty most writers have in describing personal traits accurately, the list needs to be far more than a catalogue of characteristics to be reviewed.

It should also incorporate a vocabulary supplement, and, if necessary, a glossary as well. Roget's *Thesaurus of English Words and Phrases* is invaluable in drawing up such a list.

Working with the list as a guide, the writer will be expected to give a pen portrait of his subject that will project into the minds of his readers a picture of a sentient human being.

In drawing up the list, the compiler must bear in mind the purpose and the extent of the appraisal, and then list the facets to be covered. Inevitably, there will be aspects of each facet that will need further consideration and will warrant additional sub-headings. The next step is to devise a vocabulary to describe them, comprising lists of words that may be applicable to each consideration. Given the ideas and the words to express them, the writer should then be considerably helped in making his assessment. Like all human systems, however, this has its weaknesses. The first is that the words in the vocabulary may become mere substitutes for the ticks and crosses on the form. A person may be labelled this or that without any real attempt to assess him. The second is that the list may become an invitation to verbosity and a temptation to glorify the writer rather than to present the subject in a true light.

Given, however, an understanding of these dangers by the writers, and a modicum of writing ability, the check list system should produce far better reports on personnel than pro formas usually do.

EXAMPLE OF LIST OF PERSONAL CHARACTERISTICS AND SUPPLEMENTARY VOCABULARIES

Note: The list and vocabularies may be extended to suit particular backgrounds and purposes.

	Positives	Negatives
ALERTNESS	Active	Apathetic
	Discreet	Dull
	Heedful	Heedless
	Impressive	Impassive
	Lively	Indifferent

	Positives	*Negatives*
	Perceptive	Lukewarm
	Prudent	Soulless
	Sensitive	Spiritless
	Wary	Thick-skinned
	Watchful	Unresponsive
ANALYTICAL ABILITY	Accurate	Blundering
	Explicit	Complicated
	Mathematical	Disjointed
	Methodical	Erroneous
	Meticulous	Indefinite
	Orderly	Inexact
	Penetrative	Mixed-up
	Precise	Obscure
	Punctilious	One-sided
	Scientific	Unsystematic
APPEARANCE	Dandified	Clumsy
	Dapper	Hard-featured
	Dashing	Ordinary
	Elegant	Rough
	Jaunty	Rude
	Natty	Slovenly
	Neat	Uncouth
	Refined	Ungainly
	Smart	Unsightly
	Spruce	Untidy
APPLICATION	Brisk	Capricious
	Busy	Dawdling
	Consistent	Dilatory
	Diligent	Easy-going
	Hard-working	Languid
	Indefatigable	Lazy
	Industrious	Slow
	Sedulous	Slack

	Positives	Negatives
	Speedy	Sleepy
	Untiring	Sluggish
CONTROL	Commanding	Gentle
	Domineering	Indecisive
	Executive	Indulgent
	Harsh	Lax
	Masterful	Lenient
	Powerful	Loose
	Rigorous	Mild
	Stern	Passive
	Strict	Soft
	Strong	Submissive
	Tyrannical	Tolerant
	Unflappable	Unresistant
EXPRESSION – written	Clear	Ambiguous
	Concise	Circumlocutory
	Explicit	Confused
	Fluent	Copious
	Laconic	Involved
	Lucid	Long-winded
	Pithy	Obscure
	Precise	Prolix
	Readable	Rambling
	Succinct	Vague
	Terse	Verbose
speech	Articulate	Accented
	Clear	Faltering
	Effusive	Impeded
	Eloquent	Inarticulate
	Loquacious	Mumbling
	Refined	Muttering
	Talkative	Spluttering
	Vocal	Stuttering

	Positives	Negatives
INITIATIVE	Bold	Dozy
	Confident	Inactive
	Energetic	Inert
	Enterprising	Indolent
	Intrepid	Lethargic
	Persevering	Listless
	Pushing	Resourceless
	Venturesome	Slothful
JUDGEMENT	Acute	Fatuous
	Astute	Foolish
	Broad	Imprudent
	Clear-sighted	Incompetent
	Discerning	Indiscreet
	Intelligent	Irrational
	Mature	Muddle-headed
	Penetrative	Obtuse
	Rational	Short-sighted
	Shrewd	Stupid
	Well-balanced	Unwise
RELATIONSHIPS	Co-operative	Antagonistic
	Cordial	Cross-purposed
	Familiar	Discordant
	Friendly	Disliked
	Harmonious	Disputatious
	Helpful	Loathed
	Obliging	Interfering
	Respected	Malicious
	Respectful	Over-familiar
	Sociable	Quarrelsome
	Understanding	Spiteful

VII REPORTS ON MEETINGS

1. A WIDESPREAD REQUIREMENT

Many kinds of staff, serving industry, commerce, local government and statutory organisations, are expected to write reports on meetings, formal and informal. The occasions may perhaps be those of exploratory talks, reviews of progress, or periodic committee or council meetings. The written requirements may vary from verbatim reports (or as near to them as the report writer can manage) to brief minutes recording the items considered and the decisions taken.

Reporting meetings is an exacting task requiring not only the ability to write quickly, but also an analytical turn of mind and, when it comes to writing the report, experience, discretion and tact. There may be times when the report writer has to walk the tight-rope between what a member meant to say, and what he actually said. More than one public speaker has been grateful to a reporter for correcting him in print. Above all, the reporter has to develop the art of careful listening and of concentrating on the job in hand.

He has, moreover, to ensure that he has all the information he needs before the committee disperses (including the names and titles of the members or representatives), and he has to identify quickly, from his notes, the extra queries he needs to settle. For example, he may not have understood the wording of a resolution, or not have heard a name that was mentioned; or perhaps he is convinced a speaker said 'May' when he meant 'June'. To try to carry all queries in one's head is folly. They should be starred or otherwise marked up in one's notes and gone through at the end of the meeting with those 'in the know'.

2. VERBATIM REPORTS

A verbatim, or near verbatim, report is required when every word that is uttered is likely to be of consequence later. Reports on interviews with people liable for prosecution are examples of this. Such interviews usually have the advantage of proceeding at the pace of the notemaker. Verbatim reports are not, however, limited to interviews. They are sometimes required for business and professional purposes, and, although tape recorders are now widely used for accuracy's sake, someone still has to produce the report in acceptable written form. For this, the skilled shorthand reporter has no equal, for he can 'see' the report unfolding and make adjustments as he goes along.

There are occasions when a full report, something less than verbatim, is needed. It is surprising how proficient people can become, with practice, in the use of the new abbreviated hands or their own abbreviations, even though they cannot write traditional shorthand. The secret for many is, of course, to write the report as soon as possible after the meeting, for memory fades quickly.

When a report is presented verbatim it is set out somewhat as follows:

DOWNE VALLEY PROTECTION SOCIETY

Report of Meeting held at Chumley Secondary School on 12 May 1981. *Present:* Mr J. W. Duncuff (chairman), Mr T. A. Lewk, Mrs L. M. Noe (etc. . . .) *Apologies for absence from:* Mr J. Neverthere and Miss S. O. Slow.

Item 1   MINUTES: Mr H. Knutt, Secretary, read out the minutes of the meeting held on 14 March. Mr T. Kee proposed and Mr L. Rye seconded that they be adopted as a correct record. This was carried unanimously.

Item 2   DOWNE VALLEY MOTORWAY
Mr T. A. Lewk: I wish to draw members' attention to reports in the Press on Friday, April 30, of the proposed line of the Downe Valley Motorway. If implemented, this

scheme will have the effect of cutting our community in half, leaving only two underpasses for traffic between the parts. It will mean, among other things, that the heavily populated eastern side of Oxley will be cut off from the open spaces on the west of the motorway; that a great swathe of demolition will rob our community of some of its most useful buildings, including the Town Lane Secondary School for 2,000 pupils completed only eight years ago: and that many people who live in West Ward and work in East Ward will be greatly inconvenienced. I feel we must act without delay to bring all possible pressure to bear on the Ministry and on the County to have the line altered. Accordingly, I wish to move, Mr Chairman, that we call a public meeting to protest against the proposal, to form an Action Committee and to press for a deputation to meet the Minister as soon as possible.

Members: Hear, hear!

Mrs Noe: I wish to second the motion, Mr Chairman, and to put in a special plea on behalf of the mothers of young children. It is hard enough for many of them to get the children to school as it is, but if this line goes through, many of those in West Ward will have to trail as much as a mile extra to take the children to school. I think the scheme is diabolical! Why can't the motorway be taken over Humbolds Moor instead of through this narrow valley? (etc. . . .)

Notice that the speeches are given exactly as delivered (though some tidying up is allowed for the sake of clarity, grammar or syntax). Therefore there is no need to use quotation marks.

3. REPORTED SPEECH

Far more common than verbatim reports are those where the device called Reported Speech is used. In Reported Speech the tenses of the original are moved, as it were, one stage further back, and the pronouns are changed. This form of reporting requires a little practice at first, but is fairly easy and has two big advantages:

(a) The reporter does not have to use the exact words of the speaker so long as the meaning is the same.

(b) He need give only the gist or a summary of what was said.

Hence a report of Item 2 of the Downe Valley Protection Society meeting could have been presented in Reported Speech as follows:

Item 2 DOWNE VALLEY MOTORWAY

Mr T. A. Lewk referred to Press reports concerning the proposed line for the Downe Valley Motorway. He said that the scheme, if implemented, would cut Oxley in two; would seriously impair the town's amenities; would mean the demolition of many buildings, including the new Town Lane Secondary School; and would cause great inconvenience to workers who lived in West Ward and worked in East Ward. He proposed the calling of a public protest meeting to form an Action Committee and to press for a meeting with the Minister without delay.

Mrs Noe, seconding the motion, put in a special plea for mothers who would have to walk much further to take their children to school. Why not take the motorway over Humbolds Moor? she asked.

4. MINUTES

All meetings require an official record of proceedings, called Minutes, kept by the clerk, or secretary. Minutes are not reports. They are a record of the items discussed and of the decisions taken. Usually they are in two parts: first, an outline of the subject discussed; secondly, the resolution. Minutes do not normally include the names of proposers and seconders, (though they may be included if necessary), nor do they include amendments that were abortive. Generally speaking, the more formal the meeting, the more economical the minutes.

It is customary for the original of the minutes to be kept by the clerk or secretary in a Minute Book, and for copies to be circulated to members along with the agenda for the next meeting. After any apologies for absence, the first item considered by a committee or council is the minutes of the previous meeting. These may be 'taken as read', or they may be read out. In either case, they have to be approved by the meeting as a correct record of proceedings, and, as such, signed by the chairman. Hence the need for the greatest care in drawing up the minutes of a meeting. A secretary who gets the facts wrong, or who puts a wrong interpretation on a committee decision, will find his work strongly criticised at the next meeting. Often his task is made more difficult by members' own ineptitude. People do not always say what they mean. It is up to the chairman or the secretary, therefore, to spell out exactly the form a resolution will take, before it is put to the vote. Failure to do this can lead to much argument later.

Each minute is numbered serially throughout the Minute Book and has its own heading.

In the make up of Minutes, there are one or two introductory phrases or clauses useful to the secretary. They include:

The Clerk referred to . . .

The Chief Engineer reported on . . . (*or* that . . .)

Mr H. O. Quest raised the question of . . .

The Secretary submitted a statement by . . .

The Clerk read out a letter from . . .

The Chairman commented on . . .

The Committee considered . . .

The Committee reviewed . . .

These form introductions to the first part of a minute and are followed by a brief outline of the item considered by the Committee. How long that outline shall be is a matter for discretion.

The second part of the minute records the decision taken. If the committee does not possess executive powers, the usual introductory form is:

RECOMMENDED: that . . .

If the committee has executive powers this becomes:

RESOLVED: that . . .

Even where a committee decides to take no action, its decision must be recorded.

Examples of minutes are:

1 MINUTES

> *Resolved:* That the minutes of the meeting held on May 12 1981 (a copy of which has been sent to each member of the committee) be taken as read and signed by the chairman as a correct record.

26 SUTTON MOSS DRAINAGE

The Chief Engineer submitted a progress report on works undertaken in the Sutton Moss drainage scheme during the period 1 January to 31 March. He referred to delays caused by frost and snow, and requested permission to recruit more labour to speed up the work.

> *Resolved:* That the report be received and that extra labour be recruited.

41 NEW CURTAINS

The Chairman spoke of the need to renew the velvet curtains at the windows of the Council Chamber. The present curtains were extremely faded, and were threadbare in places.

> *Resolved:* That tenders be invited for the provision of new curtains.

54 PINFOLD FOUNDRY

The Public Health Inspector reported that complaints had been received of grit, dust and fumes emanating from these premises. After investigations, an assurance had been received that equipment would be changed within a month and this would remove the cause of the grit and dust. Further investigations were being made with a view to reducing the fumes.

> *Resolved:* That the report be received and the situation be kept under review.

SECTION 4

ENGLISH FOR REPORT WRITERS

I APPLYING THE LANGUAGE

1. THE MEDIUM

English is one language – but it has many applications, each calling for a different approach and a different style. There is the language of poetry and that of the limerick; the language of elegant prose and that of slang; the language of the nursery and that of the sixth form; the language of the workshop and that of the boardroom. What is suitable and good communication in one setting or context will not be suitable or good communication in another. What makes 'Drinka pinta milka day' such a success on a hoarding will make it a source of irritation and failure in a serious article on a serious topic.

That English is capable of many different styles and usages and that there are modes of expression appropriate to each, is one of the first lessons a writer has to learn. The knowledge will save him from excesses of floweriness or pedantry on the one hand, and of triteness or colloquialism on the other. Having recognised that we all use our language differently according to circumstances, he will begin to ask himself what are the determining factors in each style or usage, and why one mode is more appropriate for one application than it is for another. Why, for example, do we accept 'Beanz meanz Heinz' as good communication on a hoarding when we would writhe at it in formal writing? The answer is that hoarding messages have to be short, clever and catchy, and the Heinz message is all three. It breaks the rules both of spelling and of grammar, but these shortcomings are overlooked because the message succeeds. English has been made to serve the ends of the Adman.

Similarly, though by no means with the same result, English must be made to serve the ends of the report writer. Two considerations largely decide the style and the usage he adopts. They are his purpose and his readership. The report writer's purpose is to present the facts in as simple, straightforward and concise a manner as possible, using words and terms he knows his readers will understand. He is not merely writing; he is communicating at a certain level and in a certain vein. His readers do not wish to be entertained or titillated; they wish to be informed as quickly, easily and painlessly as possible. Some of the considerations that make for ease of understanding in report writing have already been touched upon, such as thorough preparation, step by step presentation and good layout. However, it is at the level of language that most difficulties occur and most obscurities arise. To write simply is harder than most people are prepared to admit, and to do it with style is harder still.

2. SIMULTANEOUS DEMANDS

Few mental activities make so many simultaneous demands upon the mind as writing does. Conversation is ephemeral and transient; writing is in black and white for as long as ever the print shall last. In speech there is feed-back and two sentences may be quickly uttered to do the service of one. In writing, the writer glances continually over his shoulder wondering what the reader's reactions may be. The resultant uncertainty or embarrassment is enough to stiffen the style and impede the flow of some writers. Then there is the matter of expression. Ideas, formulated in the mind of the writer with greater or lesser precision, have to be expressed in words which are themselves imprecise, but which must be so chosen and combined as to mirror the thought and advance the argument of the writer. Yet all must be written with flair and imagination as by a person, and not mathematically and mechanically, as by a machine. Moreover what is written must be disciplined by the rules of grammar and of syntax, governed by the task in hand and modified by a consideration of the readers' needs. Small wonder there is no panacea for poor writing!

Communication is a many-sided activity in which one person may observe all the rules and yet not achieve success, and another may seem to break them and yet achieve the result he requires. Amidst the welter of considerations that contribute to success in writing, it would be a bold teacher indeed who claimed to know how to overcome the problems of communication. The hints that follow are a few which, it is hoped, will help readers of this book to achieve greater felicity in writing clearly, concisely and cogently.

II UNITS OF EXPRESSION

1. CRAFTSMANSHIP

The experienced writer may be likened to a craftsman who has certain materials which he uses to produce a desired effect. The builder uses brick, stone, steel, concrete and wood to erect an edifice according to the plan laid down. The writer uses words, phrases, sentences, paragraphs and chapters to construct the edifice of his report. Just as the builder is skilled in the handling of his materials, so the experienced writer is skilled in the handling of his. It is part of the apprenticeship of writing to learn how to handle the 'bricks' of the trade; how to build up units of expression into a complete communication. Taking words, phrases, sentences, paragraphs and chapters as the units, the writer learns the properties of each and the qualities to be borne in mind when using them to express what needs to be said.

2. WORDS

English is a double language, the result of a marriage of convenience between Anglo-Saxon, a Germanic language, and Norman-French, a Latin language. If one had to attribute personality to each, then Anglo-Saxon might be likened to the male for its strength and directness and Norman-French to the female for its charm and subtlety. Anglo-Saxon words are shorter and more easily understood; they are the words used most in ordinary conversation. French words are usually longer and are harder for people to understand but they bring with them a truly Latin comprehensiveness. Hence, the smaller a person's vocabulary in English, the more likely is it that the majority of the words he knows are of Anglo-Saxon origin. As his vocabulary grows, words of Latin origin increase until they finally preponderate.

Because English is a double language it combines in a most

effective way simplicity, strength and subtlety. The art of the writer is to achieve the correct 'mix' for the purpose he has in mind. In time past there has often been an excessive use of words of Latin origin in serious writing, probably because most writers and their readers had some form of classical education or because they were aping their 'betters'.

Nowadays, largely as a result of popular literature and journalism, there is a swing in the opposite direction. Today the emphasis is on choosing short, familiar words, which are almost certain to be Anglo-Saxon. As in all popular movements, however, the swing may go too far. There is more to writing good, lucid English than choosing short words. The adoption of an Anglo-Saxon basic English can only result in a great impoverishment of writing. The skilled writer chooses the short word for its simplicity and directness and the longer word for its subtlety or precision, as occasion requires.

The following introductory list is an indication of a few of the choices that face the writer in English.

Long	*Short*
Abbreviate	Shorten
Commence	Begin
Consider	Think
Despatch	Send
Accelerate	Quicken
Accoutrement	Outfit
Acrimonious	Bitter
Agriculture	Farming
Altitude	Height
Ameliorate	Better
Ambulant	Walking
Amicable	Friendly
Amount	Sum

In making his choice, the writer must remember that words are seldom wholly synonymous. Even though two words may be said to mean the same thing, we will apply them differently. For example, altitude means height; but we would never write, 'John's altitude is 1m 80cm'. When selecting a word, the writer

H.T.W.R.--F

bears in mind not only its meaning, but also its usage in the context intended for it. Such considerations are a matter of idiom. They make the choice of words in any language difficult for the inexperienced.

The aim of the writer should be constantly to enlarge and to improve his vocabulary until he is able to choose with ease the precise word that will convey his meaning exactly and economically. Not for him the boast of the after-dinner speaker who rose to his feet and said:

'Gentlemen, as you all know I am a man of few words . . . but I do tend to use them over and over again!'

Two practices make for a sound vocabulary. They are:

(a) wide and constant reading;

(b) unstinted use of a good dictionary.

Neglect of either is bound to reduce the capabilities of the report writer.

3. PHRASES AND CLAUSES

Phrases should be apt, clear and concise. Much writing is unnecessarily verbose, employing long phrases and clauses that could easily be reduced to one or two words. Examples of circumlocutions to be avoided are:

(a) *It . . . that*

It is clear that . . .	clearly . . .
It is obvious that . . .	obviously . . .
It is apparent that . . .	apparently . . .
It is presumed that . . .	presumably . . .

(b) *Fact*

In view of the fact that . . .	as . . .
Because of the fact that . . .	because . . .
Except for the fact that . . .	except that . . .
Aware of the fact that . . .	aware that . . .

(c) *Field, realm, nature*

In the field of engineering	in engineering
In the realms of politics	in politics
Of a stony nature	stony

(d) *Verb plus noun*

Offer an observation	observe
Make an application	apply
Tender resignation	resign
Give a report	report
Take into consideration	consider
Effect a saving	save

(e) *Double verb*

Causes to deflect	deflects

(f) *Euphemism*

Suffering an indisposition	ill
Passed away	died
Terminated his employment	sacked him
Withdrew their labour	struck

(g) *Miscellaneous*

During the course of	during
For the purpose of	for
In the first place	firstly
In most instances	mostly
In few instances	seldom, rarely, occasionally
In the direction of	towards
In the near future	soon
At present	now
At that time	then
In the event that	should
Onward transmission	forwarding

(h) *Tautology*

Ascend up	ascend
Attach together	attach
Co-operate together	co-operate
Follow after	follow
New innovation	innovation
Return back	return
Revert back	revert
Circle round	circle
Continue to remain	remain
Original source	source

4. SENTENCES

In general, sentences of not more than twenty to twenty-five words may be taken as the norm. Short sentences are more easily assimilated than long and they lessen the likelihood of either the writer or the reader losing his way. The twenty-five word limit, however, like motor car speed limits, may sometimes be observed more in the breach than in practice. Sentences are discrete statements expressing sometimes one idea, sometimes several, whose combination, relationship or subordination are essential to convey precisely the reasoning or the sentiments the writer has in mind. (There are, for example, thirty-one words in the last sentence!) The point is that the report writer should keep down the length of his sentences except when the proper statement of his thought demands otherwise.

Sentences are broadly classified into three groups:

(*a*) *Simple*

    Examples of simple sentences are:

        The dog bit the man. (transitive)

        He staggered.   (intransitive)

        'Go!' 'Help!'   (imperative)

In report writing and in technical writing generally, the commonest uses of the simple sentence are:

    (i) for passing on instructions:

        Turn left at the traffic lights.

        Take the next right fork.

        Follow the route signposted SHIPLEY.

        Turn right at the roundabout.

        Look for the OTLEY sign.

    (ii) for making unqualified observations:

        The runner showed signs of fatigue after 20 miles.

        He was obviously distressed at 25 miles.

        He collapsed after 30 miles.

(*b*) *Compound*

    Examples of compound sentences are:

        The dog bit the man and then ran off.

        He staggered but managed to keep his balance.

'Help!' he cried, 'or I shall faint.'

Compound sentences are simple sentences joined by such words as *and, but, for, so* and *or*. Such sentences are for expressing co-ordinate ideas which, when joined, imply progression, comparison, contrast or balance. If there is no such co-ordination, the ideas should not be expresssd in the same sentence.

'He joined the firm in 1963 and rose to be manager in eight years,' has an obvious co-ordination.

'He joined the firm in 1963 and married in 1971;' has not, unless he married the boss's daughter.

(*c*) *Complex*

Although the runner showed signs of fatigue after 20 miles, he did not begin to show distress until after 25 miles.

is an example of a complex sentence. In such sentences one idea, or even several ideas, may be subordinated to the principal idea, as in:

Although the runner had trained hard, and was supplied with glucose drinks along the route, he showed signs of fatigue after 20 miles. Despite his distress, he struggled on until the 30-mile mark, where he collapsed.

In complex sentences there is scope for intricacies of thought and nuances of meaning that cannot be expressed in either simple or compound sentences. For that reason, complex sentences demand greater skill in writing to ensure that the required shade of meaning is conveyed.

5. PARAGRAPHS

The traditional concept of the paragraph is that it is a group of associated sentences defining and developing one aspect of a subject. Paragraphs may be used to:

(*a*) introduce;

(*b*) develop;

(*c*) define;

(*d*) explain;

    (*e*) describe;

    (*f*) classify;

    (*g*) compare;

    (*h*) summarise;

    (*j*) conclude.

In this, however, as in other writing concepts, ideas are changing. Popular journalism long ago seized upon short paragraphs as a means of lightening the appearance of the text and of making it more easily digestible. Technical writing is following suit, though it generally shows more restraint in jettisoning long paragraphs. Whether to use short paragraphs or long depends largely upon readership and upon the subject matter. Serious, closely-knit exposition requires longer paragraphs if the aspects are to be dealt with coherently. Explanation, items in sequence, and straightforward narrative lend themselves more easily to the shorter style.

Where longer paragraphs are used, the writer should state in the first sentence the aspect to be dealt with, and should link it securely, by means of a key word or words, with what he has written in the preceding paragraphs. If the work has been carefully planned and classified, the headings themselves provide the topics or aspects to be dealt with in the first sentences of the paragraphs of the report.

6. CHAPTERS

A chapter is a main division of a piece of writing. How long it shall be varies from piece to piece. Among the deciding factors are:

    (*a*) the length of the report;

    (*b*) the number of areas of investigation;

    (*c*) the layout;

    (*d*) the style of presentation.

As with sentences and paragraphs, mass readership now expects short 'takes'. Slabs of information, unrelieved by headings or white spaces, frighten many readers into thinking the report will prove to be heavy going. On the other hand, sub-division for sub-division's sake spoils the unity and harmony of the work. Good chapter planning enhances the logic and the presentation by underlining the major aspects of the report. Chopping into short chapters, without regard to entities, ruins the structure, destroys the proportions and puts things out of perspective.

Where reports have to be prepared to an accepted pattern, the writer is often spared the task of deciding for himself what the chapter areas or divisions shall be. Where these are not provided, the writer should take his clues from the major divisions he himself established when he classified his information.

III PUNCTUATION

1. RULE IS CLARITY

Punctuation has three main purposes:
- (*a*) to mark off completed statements (sentences);
- (*b*) to make clear the significance of a statement and of its parts;
- (*c*) to help the reader to grasp the meaning rapidly and easily.

The rule of punctuation is clarity. Views differ on the precise application of punctuation marks, but the general principles are, in the main, agreed.

2. FULL STOP OR PERIOD

Marks off each sentence (each complete, discrete statement). Sentences vary greatly in length. The shortest is the imperative form, as in 'Go!'

Note: 'Having come all this way . . . ' is not a sentence because it is not a discrete statement, i.e. it will not stand on its own.

3. COMMA

Indicates a brief pause. It is used:
- (*a*) To separate items in a list of three or more:

  We packed clips, tubes, nuts, bolts and bars (note the omission of the comma before 'and').

  We bought ham, beef, pork, pickles, bread, and butter (note the inclusion of the comma before 'and', since the bread was not buttered).
- (*b*) To mark off any phrase or clause that interrupts the flow of a sentence:

  We can complete the work, provided there is no mechanical breakdown, by Wednesday morning.

(c) To differentiate between clauses that define and those that
are a comment:

The Company *which won the Queen's award* has put on a
fine exhibition (defining).

The Company, *which won the Queen's award,* has put on a
fine exhibition (commenting).

(d) To mark off co-ordinate phrases or clauses:

The scheme did not, and still does not, apply to salary
earners.

(e) To mark off titles or identifiers:

Mr James Smith, managing director, said ...

4. SEMI-COLON

A useful, though neglected, device whose function lies between
that of the comma and of the full stop. It is used:

(a) To mark off phrases (especially in lists) in which the comma
already appears:

The soldiers were transported by road; the specialists, by
helicopter; the refugees, by river craft.

(b) To balance ideas within a sentence:

He declines work; he refuses charity.

(c) To enable a sentence to be extended without breaking the
unity:

The phrase will have little effect upon the reader; by then
he will be conditioned by it.

(d) To list subject matter, as in Terms of Reference:

An investigation into electromagnetic interference originat-
ing from radio amateur transmitters; the technical causes;
means of control; the views of the amateur; the views of
complainants; and the responsibility of the manufacturers
of equipment.

5. COLON

Is used:

(a) To introduce a series of items:

The camper's needs are: tent, groundsheet, cooking utensils, stove, sleeping-bag and waterproof clothing.

(*b*) To introduce an explanatory statement:

This is the Company's plan: to open a new factory in Belgium and so save the costs of transporting goods to the Continent.

(*c*) For contrast:

A quick temper causes strife: a soft answer turns away wrath.

(*d*) In place of the comma, to introduce a quotation:

Witness: 'I was not there.'

6. DASH

Is used:

(*a*) Instead of a bracket to indicate a parenthesis:

The lorries – there were three of them – all came round the corner on the wrong side.

(*b*) To indicate an additional thought:

Wilkins arrived late – a sure sign that his car would not start.

(*c*) Where a word is repeated, together with an explanation:

The strike will have serious effects for all – effects upon transport workers, upon service employees, upon employment in kindred trades.

(*d*) After a series where a summary is introduced by *all* or *these*:

Dirt, squalor, poverty – all contribute to the natives' misery.

7. EXCLAMATION MARKS

Sometimes called 'screamers', should be used sparingly, one at a time, to indicate strong feeling, or the unexpected:

Whoopee!

Holden's are building a new factory – and we thought they were short of capital!

8. HYPHENS

Are hard to handle properly. They are used:

(a) To compound two nouns to form a separate word:

> life-span
> barrel-chest
> blow-hole
> coat-armour

The difficulty with such combinations is that they often merge in time, as the following have already done:

> headmaster
> armchair
> coastguard

If in doubt, therefore, consult a modern dictionary.

(b) To link adjectives, for clarity:

> a black-coated worker
> a white-collar worker
> an old type-face

(c) To compound numbers and fractions:

> ninety-nine
> two-thirds

(d) To separate the same vowel in consecutive syllables:

> re-enlist; co-operate; pre-exempt

(e) To avoid confusion between similar words:

recover	re-cover
reform	re-form
refuse	re-fuse
recollect	re-collect

(f) Sometimes with prefixes:

> all-pervasive
> anti-submarine
> auto-suggestion
> ex-chairman
> semi-detached

9. QUESTION MARKS

Are used:

(*a*) At the end of a direct question:

'What is your labour turnover?' he asked.

(*b*) Where a question is implied:

'You were showing a profit up to then?' queried the accountant.

Note: There is no question mark after an indirect question:

He asked what their labour turnover was.

The accountant asked whether they were showing a profit up to that time.

10. QUOTATION MARKS

There are two kinds: 'singles' and "doubles". Either may be used, but they must be used consistently. In marking off words actually spoken, the choice of whether to use singles before doubles, or doubles before singles, is arbitrary. Most people use doubles first:

"The supervisor said to me, 'We will be working over tonight'," said the labourer.

But it could equally well be punctuated:

'The supervisor said to me, "We will be working over tonight"，' said the labourer.

Choose your style and stick to it.

What to do with punctuation at the end of quotations is sometimes difficult to decide. The guide is commonsense. Generally the practice is to put the punctuation inside the quotes except where the sense requires otherwise, as in:

Did I hear you say, 'The supervisor told me to work over'?

Note that a question or an exclamation mark has the force of a full stop at the end of a sentence.

Single quotes are often used to enclose words used in a special sense:

The 'permanents' vied with the 'temporaries' in their production targets.

11. APOSTROPHES

Kindle controversy out of all proportion to their size. Many people would like to dispense with them altogether and are doing so – particularly in titles and notices. Clarity, however, demands that apostrophes be retained in formal writing.

Their uses are:

(a) To indicate possession:

John's book	Where the ownership
A boy's hat	is singular
Boys' gymnasium	Where the ownership
Footballers' restroom	is plural

Notes:

(i) If a word is already plural, e.g. men, children, the apostrophe stays between the last letter and the 's' as in: Men's clothing; Children's games.

(ii) The possessive pronouns *its, hers, ours, yours, theirs,* no longer carry the apostrophe.

(iii) The argument really begins over words ending in s. Shall it be Keats' poetry, or Keats's poetry? How people say it, is perhaps as good a guide as any. St James' Church may be all right in a notice, but 'I go to St James's' is what most parishioners would say.

(iv) In the case of words ending in -ses, -sis, -sus the omission of the final 's' in the possessive is common: Moses' law, Ulysses' adventures.

(b) To indicate that a letter has been omitted: Don't; It's (= it is).

(c) In plurals of numbers and letters: Two 6's; Three S's. *Note:* The letter itself usually appears in capitals, and is not quoted as in 'S's'.

12. DOTS

Are often used to signify a break in a quotation. They should be suitably spaced and should not number more than three:

Not only should all four tyres be of the same type . . . but also, for maximum safety, they should be of the same make.

IV SOME POINTS TO WATCH

A AND AN

A is used before consonants, including *h*, on most occasions when the *h* is sounded:

> a hug, a heap, a house, a horse, etc.

It is also used before a *u* sound, as in:

> a united, a European, a eucalyptus, a unicorn.

AN is used before other vowels and diphthongs, and also before *h* when it is unsounded, as in:

> an hour, an honest, an heir.

Sometimes *AN* is used, for euphony's sake, before a slightly aspirated *h*, as in:

> an hotel, an historic.

ABBREVIATIONS

Every trade and profession has its jargon and its abbreviations. The danger is that the report writer may use them unthinkingly and confuse those readers who are not members of the same technical club. Often a reasonable compromise is to give the full title at the first mention and to use the abbreviation thereafter. If there are many abbreviations or unfamiliar technical terms, a glossary should be provided.

Some abbreviations become words in their own right, such as:

> UNESCO: United Nations Educational Scientific and Cultural Organisation.
>
> ASLEF: Associated Society of Locomotive Engineers and Firemen.

They are then called acronyms. They still need an explanation for most readers. Note that stops do not appear between the letters of an acronym.

ACTIVE AND PASSIVE

There are two voices in English:

Active: The man struck the boy.

Passive: The boy was struck by the man.

Two things are immediately obvious from a comparison of these two sentences:

(*a*) the active is the more direct;

(*b*) the passive is longer.

Many technical writers are in the habit of writing in the passive as a result of years of writing Laboratory or Test reports, for which the accepted style is: Third Person; Past Tense; Passive Voice. Nowadays the use of a more personal and active style is less frowned upon and is even being encouraged in some quarters. Instead of:

Two samples of a material were taken and tested to destruction;

one reads:

I (or we) took two samples of the material and tested them to destruction.

The danger is, of course, that the total adoption of the active means, for some writers, the continual insertion of the pronouns *I* or *We*, which becomes both tedious and tiresome for the reader. Perhaps a sensible course is to use a mixture of both active and passive to keep the report alive and crisp, and to put the emphases in the proper places. Where, for example, the name of the person who carried out a particular task may be relevant because of his experience or specialist knowledge, why not say, actively, that he did the work?:

Mr Henry Smith, our senior engineer, supervised the installation of the new plant.

ADOPT AND ADAPT

Are sometimes confused:

To Adopt means to take or use as one's own, as in:

The firm adopted the new method and increased its output by 50 per cent.

To Adapt means to modify for a particular purpose, as in:

The firm adapted the new method to its own processes and increased output by 50 per cent.

AFFECT AND EFFECT
Frequently give trouble:

Affect is a verb. It means either:
  (a) to act upon and produce change, as in:
      The disappointment did not affect his performance.
or (b) to pretend, as in:
      He affected ignorance, although he knew a great deal about the subject.

Effect is both a noun and a verb.
  (a) As a noun it means the result of an action, as in:
      The huge dose of poison had little effect upon Rasputin.
  (b) As a verb it means to carry out or to accomplish, as in:
      The new manager effected a big improvement in production.

AMPERSAND (&)
The ampersand sign should not be used in reports, though it is a useful abbreviation when one is making notes.

ALTERNATELY
Means by turns, as in:
A cyclist presses the pedals alternately to propel the machine.

ALTERNATIVELY
Implies a choice, as in:
We can travel by air, or, alternatively, by sea.

ALTERNATIVES
Are limited to two at a time. There cannot be three, four, or more alternatives.

ANTICIPATE

Is not the same as *expect*. To anticipate is to take up, or to act, beforehand, as in:

We anticipated the rival firm's plans by producing a new model three months before they did. We expect (not anticipate) the work will keep us busy for two years.

BECAUSE

Is often used redundantly where a reason is being offered, as in:

The reason for his failure was *because* he would not work.

This should read:

The reason for his failure was *that* he would not work.

BETWEEN

Relates to two objects. If there are more than two, use *among*:

The goalkeeper crouched *between* the posts.

The ball sailed high over his head and was lost *among* the spectators.

BESIDE

Means 'at the side of', as in the song:

'I do like to be beside the seaside . . . '

BESIDES

Means 'in addition to', as in:

Someone else, besides the accused, must have falsified the accounts.

CAPITALS

The modern trend is away from the excessive use of initial capitals. They are retained for:

(*a*) *Proper names*

the Firth of Forth

Magna Carta

the Battle of Waterloo.

(b) *Full titles*
> the Royal Society of Arts
> the British Association of Industrial Editors.

Note that, in subsequent references, the shorter forms:
> the society
> the association

may be used without the initial capital, unless there is a likelihood of confusion with another society or association.

(c) *Holders of office or position*
> the Chairman of the Council
> the Managing Director

Here again, shorter references sometimes appear without the initial capital:
> the chairman
> the managing director.

COLLECTIVE NOUNS

First decide whether you are to treat a collective noun as an entity (in which case it will be singular), or as a group whose members are acting individually (in which case it will be plural). Then try to abide by your decision through the thick and thin of verbal agreements:

> *Singular:* The company has decided on computerisation and has sent its managers on a course.
>
> *Plural:*   The army are on the lookout for arms smugglers.

Watch out for the trap sprung by the pronouns, *its* and *theirs*, and thus avoid such errors as:

> The company *has* decided on computerisation. *Their* managers are attending a course next month.
>
> The group *are* holding a conference in London to ensure that all sales personnel are aware of *its* plans for the future.

COMPRISE

Means 'to contain' or 'to include'. It does not take the preposition 'of':

> The estate comprises (not *of*) three farms, six cottages and two hundred acres of arable land.

CONTRACTIONS

Such as:

    it's   = it is
    don't   = do not
    I've   = I have

should not be used in formal writing.

DUE TO

Means 'caused by', and is often confused with *owing to*, which means 'because of':

    The fall in sales, due to market uncertainty, came at a most inconvenient time.

    Owing to the recession, 200 employees were declared redundant.

Note that *owing to* could have been used in both these sentences; *Due to* in only the first.

FEWER

Refers to number; *less* refers to size. Hence:

    Less cans of beer were drunk last year.

would be correct only if the cans were smaller.

    Fewer cans of beer were drunk last year.

is improbable, but grammatically correct.

FOLLOWING

Is not a substitute for *after*.

    Following the war, he joined the Post Office as an engineer.

is incorrect because the man was not a camp follower when he joined the Post Office. He was a discharged soldier who joined the Post Office after completing his military service.

INFER

Is often confused with *imply*, as in:

    What do you infer by that remark?

which should read:

    What do you imply by that remark?

To infer is to deduce, as in:

From his conversation, I inferred that he was an engineer.
To imply is to suggest, or to insinuate, as in:

His words implied that the company was not being managed efficiently.

-IZE AND -ISE

Scholars tell us that the correct form of the word ending, etymologically, is -ize. The difficulty is that some words are seldom, if ever, spelt that way, such as:

advertise, sympathise, compromise, supervise and televise

So I would advise (there it is again!) the adoption of the *-ise* form, which is the more popular in this country, and which poses no problems. If, however, the writer wishes to follow the pedants, without compromize, he may do so.

LICENCE AND LICENSE

Licence is the noun – the piece of paper, the authority to do something – as in:

He held a licence to drive the heavy goods vehicle.

License is the verb – the granting of the authority – as in:

He was licensed to drive the heavy goods vehicle.

LIE AND LAY

To lie is to rest or to recline. It is intransitive, that is to say it cannot carry the action over to an object. One cannot *lie* anything. *To lay* is to set down. It is a transitive verb, that is to say it carries the action over to an object. Hence one can lay bricks, railway lines – even ghosts! And, of course, hens can lay eggs.
Examples of the use of the two verbs are:

The doctor told the patient to lie (not lay) on the couch.
Snow lies (not lays) on the northern slope of the mountain throughout the summer.
The workman was asked to lay (not lie) his tools on the bench.

LIKE

Is increasingly being used, incorrectly, as a substitute for *as* or *as if*:

Do like he does and you will not go far wrong.

which should read:

Do as he does and you will not go far wrong.

Similarly:

He behaves like he was boss around here.

should read:

He behaves as if he was boss around here.

LISTING

Is good practice in technical writing. It avoids long explanations and aids assimilation. Usually the list is introduced by a governing clause, such as:

Recommendations in a report should be:

and then follows the list. There is a danger, however, that the writer may lose sight of the governing verb as the list grows, with the result that the items are not, as we say, parallel. Here is an example of the fault:

Recommendations in a report should be:

- (*a*) sound;
- (*b*) well-defined;
- (*c*) consider the feelings of the persons affected;
- (*d*) include a statement of the cost.

In this list, items (*a*) and (*b*) follow on after the governing verb, whereas items (*c*) and (*d*) do not. Either the governing clause should end at the word 'should' and the word 'be' should be carried over to introduce the first two items, or the last two items should be re-written to comply with the governing verb.

LOCATE

Means 'to place', not 'to find'. Therefore:

The typist left the letters on the desk, where the manager was sure to locate them.

is wrong.

MATTER

Can be vague. It is better to be precise and state what the 'matter' is, e.g. a complaint, request, letter, loss . . .

MEDIA

Is the plural of medium when it is used in the sense of intervening agencies, e.g. the mass media when referring to newspapers, television, radio. A medium is a spiritualist, intermediary, or, sometimes, a size.

MIXED METAPHOR

Metaphors require careful handling in report writing. Slippery slopes, bottlenecks, targets, blow-by-blow accounts, may give a certain raciness of style to reports, but they have a nasty habit of getting mixed up, or of imparting a meaning the writer has not foreseen. Consider, for example, these three sentences from an article in an American magazine on, of all subjects, 'Communication':

> 'Take *the field* of selling. At *the top of the ladder* you will find a great many people in it: sales managers, vice-presidents for sales, etc. As you go *down the ranks*, however, it becomes difficult to find people in this *line of work*.'

All up the creek!

ONLY

Is a short word that is frequently misplaced. Generally speaking it should be placed immediately before the word it is intended to qualify. Consider, for example, the changes of meaning resulting from the alteration of the position of the word *only* in the following sentences:

> Only he went down the road (he was the only person to do so).
> He only went down the road (that was all he did).
> He went only down the road (and not up it).
> He went down only the road (not the footpath, or the avenue).
> He went down the only road (there was no other to go down).

PARTICIPLES
Are verbal adjectives. When used at the beginnings of sentences, they often stay unrelated to the rest of the sentence, as in:

Sitting on top of the pyramid, the camels looked like ants.

when, in fact, the observer was on the pyramid and the camels were down below. To avoid hanging, unrelated or misrelated participles (which are all names for this fault), the writer should make it a rule that he always follows the participial phrase with the person who is performing the action, as in:

Sitting on top of the pyramid, he thought the camels looked like ants.

A second danger with participles is that they are sometimes given the status of verbs and that what is really only a participial phrase may be treated as though it were a whole sentence – full stop and all. An example of this is the hoary old letter ending:

Assuring you of our best attention at all times,

which is a participial phrase, has no verb in it, and therefore is not a sentence.

PARTIALLY
Means 'to a limited extent', as in:

The pensioner was partially handicapped as a result of war wounds.

PARTLY
Means 'in part', as in:

The strikers were partly responsible for the overall drop in production.

POSITION
Is often used as a verb where *place* would be adequate as in:

The illustration should be positioned (placed) in the centre of the text.

PRINCIPLE AND PRINCIPAL
Are often confused. *Principle* is the ethic, or code of conduct, as in:

On principle, the trade unionists refused to handle the goods the blacklegs had transported.

Principal means 'chief', either as an adjective or as a noun, as in:

A power failure was reported to be the principal reason for the delay.

The principal of the firm is a mature and efficient manager.

PRIOR TO

Is a stuffy way of saying, *before:*

Prior to his arrival, we had re-arranged the office.

PRONOUNS

Ask yourself whether a pronoun is the subject or object of the verb in the sentence. If it is the subject, it should be in the nominative case; if it is the object, in the accusative case:

Nominatives	*Accusatives*
I	me
he, she	him, her
we	us
you	you
they	them

Watch out especially for double accusatives, as in:

He gave the cake to Johnny and me (not I).

The class spoke highly of him and me (not he and I).

Treat pronouns used with the verb 'to be' with care. 'It is me', may be colloquially acceptable, but 'it is I' is grammatically correct because the verb 'To be' takes the same case (nominative) after it as before it. So:

This is he (not *him*).

These are they (not *them*).

Pronouns after prepositions are always in the accusative:

All left the stage except *him*.

There was a bond between *them* and *us*.

We have no one like *him* in the team.

After *as* and *than*, the case of a pronoun is decided by its relationship to the verb in the sentence. Repeat the verb, mentally, to find the correct form:

John can run faster than *he* (can run).

The manager liked him better than (he liked) *her*.

He cannot work as hard as *I* (can work).

REPLACE

Should not be used in technical instructions lest it should cause confusion, as in:

Replace the sprocket on the hub.

This may leave the reader uncertain as to whether he should renew the sprocket, or should put back the original.

SHALL AND WILL

To express simple future, use:

Shall with the first person, singular or plural.

Will with the second and third persons.

Examples:

I *shall* read the paper at our next conference.

We *shall* all be there to hear it.

You *will* then see the relevance of my argument.

It *will* be unanswerable.

To express force of will, or obligation, use:

Will with the first person, singular or plural.

Shall with the second and third persons.

Examples:

I *will* go myself to examine the property.

We *will* discuss the matter later.

You *shall* go at some other time.

The owner *shall* await our decision.

SIZED

Is the adjective, not *size*, as in:

Pint-*sized* (not *size*) cans.

SUCH

Is sometimes used, incorrectly, for *in such a way*, as in:

The joint was made such that it could not be fractured; which should read:

The joint was made in such a way that it could not be fractured.

UNDER THE CIRCUMSTANCES
Often appears in writing instead of 'in the circumstances'. The circumstances are the surrounding conditions; therefore the correct preposition is 'in', not 'under'.

UP UNTIL
Is an old English, but latterly an American, redundancy that is rapidly gaining ground in this country, thanks largely, but unfortunately, to TV and radio commentators. 'Until' means 'up to a certain time'; it does not heed to be bolstered (up) in this way.

UNIQUE
Means without like or equal. It cannot be compared, as in:
more unique, most unique, rather unique, very unique.

VIA
Has to do with direction, not with the mode of travel. It is therefore incorrect to write:
He went via the train to London;
when we mean:
He went by train to London (via Derby?).

INDEX

Italics indicate that the words themselves, their correct English usage, are being referred to.

Keywords

Raymond Williams

Alienation, creative, family, media, radical, structural, taste: these are seven of the hundred or so words whose derivation, development and contemporary meaning Raymond Williams explores in this unique study of the language in which we discuss 'culture' and 'Society'.

A series of connecting essays investigate how these 'keywords' have been formed, redefined, confused and reinforced as the historical contexts in which they were applied changed to give us their current meaning and significance.

'This is a book which everyone who is still capable of being educated should read.'   Christopher Hill, *New Society*

'. . . for the first time we have some of the materials for constructing a genuinely historical and a genuinely social semantics . . . Williams's book is unique in its kind so far and it provides a model as well as a resource for us all.'

Alasdair MacIntyre, *New Statesman*

Fontana Paperbacks: Non-fiction

Fontana is a leading paperback publisher of non-fiction, both popular and academic. Below are some recent titles.

- ☐ CAPITALISM SINCE WORLD WAR II Philip Armstrong, Andrew Glyn and John Harrison £4.95
- ☐ ARISTOCRATS Robert Lacey £3.95
- ☐ PECULIAR PEOPLE Patrick Donovan £1.75
- ☐ A JOURNEY IN LADAKH Andrew Harvey £2.50
- ☐ ON THE PERIMETER Caroline Blackwood £1.95
- ☐ YOUNG CHILDREN LEARNING Barbara Tizard and Martin Hughes £2.95
- ☐ THE TRANQUILLIZER TRAP Joy Melville £1.95
- ☐ LIVING IN OVERDRIVE Clive Wood £2.50
- ☐ MIND AND MEDIA Patricia Marks Greenfield £2.50
- ☐ BETTER PROGRAMMING FOR YOUR COMMODORE 64 Henry Mullish and Dov Kruger £3.95
- ☐ NEW ADVENTURE SYSTEMS FOR THE SPECTRUM S. Robert Speel £3.95
- ☐ POLICEMAN'S PRELUDE Harry Cole £1.50
- ☐ SAS: THE JUNGLE FRONTIER Peter Dickens £2.50
- ☐ HOW TO WATCH CRICKET John Arlott £1.95
- ☐ SBS: THE INVISIBLE RAIDERS James Ladd £1.95
- ☐ THE NEW SOCIOLOGY OF MODERN BRITAIN Eric Butterworth and David Weir (eds.) £2.50
- ☐ BENNY John Burrowes £1.95
- ☐ ADORNO Martin Jay £2.50
- ☐ STRATEGY AND DIPLOMACY Paul Kennedy £3.95
- ☐ BEDSIDE SNOOKER Ray Reardon £2.95

You can buy Fontana paperbacks at your local bookshop or newsagent. Or you can order them from Fontana Paperbacks, Cash Sales Department, Box 29, Douglas, Isle of Man. Please send a cheque, postal or money order (not currency) worth the purchase price plus 15p per book for postage (maximum postage required is £3).

NAME (Block letters) _____

ADDRESS _____

_____